CHEVALIER

CHEVALIER

The Films and Career of Maurice Chevalier

by
GENE RINGGOLD
and DEWITT BODEEN

Foreword by ROUBEN MAMOULIAN

THE CITADEL PRESS
Secaucus, New Jersey

ACKNOWLEDGMENTS

For the use of photographs, clippings and other courtesies, the authors wish to thank the following individuals, organizations and enterprises for their assistance:
Academy of Motion Picture Arts and Sciences Library; Antonio Alvarez; Eddie Brandt; Leonard Brown; Philip Castanza; René Clair; Oliver Dernberger; Homer Dickens; Walt Disney Productions; Allen Eyles; Robert Florey; Diane Goodrich; Pierre Guinle; Madison Lacy; Kenneth G. Lawrence; Albert Lord; Sophia Loren; Milton Luboviski; Dion MacGregor; Rouben Mamoulian; MGM; Paramount Pictures; Arthur C. Peterson; Alphonse Pintó; Dennis Preato; Charles Phillips Reilly; Francisco Rialp; Pierre Rissient; Frank Rodrigues; Larry Semler; Mildred Simpson and her staff; Charles Smith; Dorothy Textor; 20th Century-Fox Pictures; Lou Valentino; Jerry Vermilye; Warner Bros. Pictures; Malcolm Willets; and the library assistants in the Music, Newspaper and Theatre Sections of the downtown Los Angeles Public Library.
For their permission to reprint Rouben Mamoulian's tribute to Maurice Chevalier, which he elaborated for the foreword to this book, we are grateful to *The New York Times,* the publication in which part of the tribute originally appeared.

First Edition

Published by The Citadel Press,
A division of Lyle Stuart, Inc.
120 Enterprise Ave., Secaucus, N.J. 07094
In Canada: George J. McLeod Limited
73 Bathurst St., Toronto 2B, Ontario
Manufactured in the United States of America
Designed by A. Christopher Simon
Library of Congress catalog card number: 72–95413
ISBN 0–8065–0354–8

FOR HENRY HART

—who edited Films in Review *for over twenty-two years and who inspired many film historians, including the authors, to share their knowledge and love of the motion picture with others.*

CONTENTS

CHEVALIER

FOREWORD

The late 20's

The 30's

At 83, Maurice Chevalier was much too young to die. He still possessed an amazing amount of creative energy and a youth's enthusiasm for his art.

He was born the year the Eiffel Tower was built, and like it he became the symbol of Paris. Unlike it, he could travel and sing. He appeared in films and in person in most countries of the world and was embraced by every nation as partly their own.

There are singers, actors, entertainers, but there is only one Chevalier. He is unique, and being unique, he is indestructible. As a performer, he was totally integrated and the whole of him was much bigger than the sum of his various talents. His stylized silhouette, the saucy angle of his straw hat, his smile, the way he moved, sang and talked was not only artistically perfect, but spiritually uplifting to young and old. He radiated optimism, good will and above all the *joie de vivre* that every human being longs for.

Yet, when I first knew him, these qualities seemed to belong only to Chevalier, the entertainer, not the man. This was forty years ago, when I directed him in *Love Me Tonight*.

I had never witnessed such a sharp schism in any performer before. He would come on the set, slouching, sit in a corner looking as unhappy and worried as a homeless orphan. When I called him to shoot the first song, I thought it would be a disaster. He shuffled to his position, drooping head, frowning, dejected. We started the camera, I said: "Action!" and then a complete transformation took place—there he was: happy, debonaire, truly filled with that joy of living. The take was perfect. Then, as I said "Cut," the light went out of him. He walked back to his corner like a tired man, looking hopelessly miserable, as before. Through *Love Me Tonight* we became very good friends. As a person, I found him insecure and old in spirit; yet, in a way, he was also like a schoolboy in need of affection, encouragement and

The 40's

The 50's

friendship. Consciously or unconsciously, he seemed to hold the Hellenistic principle that friendship is superior to love.

The miracle of Chevalier to me, personally, was that through the forty years that followed the two natures in him, the performer and the man, became gradually integrated. As the years rolled by, he grew wiser in mind, yet truly younger at heart, fresher and gentler in spirit. Both as performer and man, he kept blossoming. He entertained generation after generation, he acted, he wrote books. The scope of his interests and enthusiasms grew wider with age.

I quote from his letter to me in September, 1968, after he had finished an incredibly arduous one-man concert tour of many countries:

> . . . Happy to have made it through sixty cities all over the world during my eightieth year . . .
>
> Now I feel my life must change and I should not run any more—just walk towards . . . what?
>
> T.V.—Big Screen—Philosophy—Reading—Writing—and admiring and loving Rouben Mamoulian.

(Hope I will be forgiven for not cutting that last—I cherish it.)

With all his development and outer sophistication, the child in him never died.

Quoting from his letter towards the end of 1970:

> . . . Entering 83 . . . Hop!

And from his last letter:

> . . . Bless you and great America.

He was truly grateful to our country and loved it. In turn, he was the best ambassador of good will that France ever had.

Many performers, artists, public figures achieve

fame, admiration, respect. But few go beyond all these and gain the ultimate tribute: the love of the people. Chevalier achieved this. The world loved him. He received this love humbly and returned it wholeheartedly. It is this love that gave him the exuberance and the energy to go through his whole life singing.

We are fortunate to have his many recordings and films that we and the future generations can enjoy. As to Chevalier himself, now that he has left us, I can see him—with his rakishly angled straw hat, his smile, his jaunty walk—singing "Mimi" to the spellbound Heavenly Host.

ROUBEN MAMOULIAN

The 60's

The 70's

MERRY WIDOW WALTZ

The MERRY WIDOW

starring
Maurice
CHEVALIER
Jeanette
MAC DONALD
In an
ERNST LUBITSCH
Merry Musical Romance

Based on Book & Lyrics
by
Victor Leon & Leo Stein

Music by Franz Lehar

New Lyrics by Lorenz Hart

A Metro-Goldwyn-Mayer
PICTURE

Other Successes
MERRY WIDOW WALTZ
GIRLS, GIRLS, GIRLS
IT MUST BE LOVE
MAXIM'S
VILIA

Music Sales Corp. Limited
21 Dundas Square
Toronto — Canada

CHAPPELL & CO., LTD.
LONDON — SYDNEY
CHAPPELL-HARMS INC.
62 WEST 45th ST.
NEW YORK, N.Y.

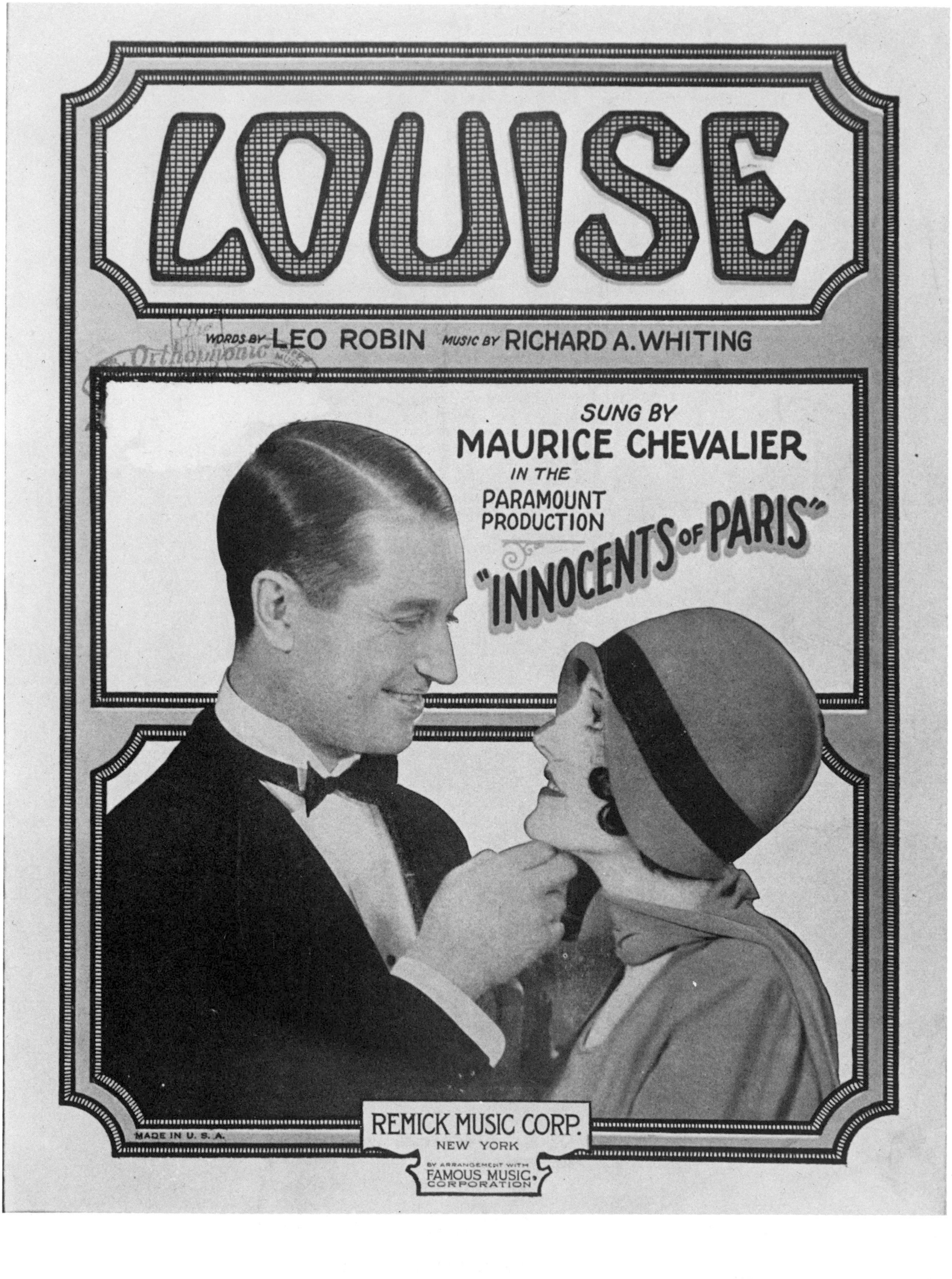
LOUISE
WORDS BY LEO ROBIN MUSIC BY RICHARD A. WHITING
SUNG BY
MAURICE CHEVALIER
IN THE
PARAMOUNT
PRODUCTION
"INNOCENTS OF PARIS"
MADE IN U. S. A.
REMICK MUSIC CORP.
NEW YORK
BY ARRANGEMENT WITH
FAMOUS MUSIC
CORPORATION

ONE HOUR WITH YOU
LYRIC BY LEO ROBIN MUSIC BY RICHARD A. WHITING
Paramount presents
MAURICE CHEVALIER
IN
AN ERNST LUBITSCH PRODUCTION
"ONE HOUR WITH YOU"
One Hour With You
We Will Always Be Sweethearts
What Would You Do
Famous Music
CORPORATION
MADE IN U.S.A.

ISN'T IT ROMANTIC?
LYRIC BY LORENZ HART • MUSIC BY RICHARD RODGERS
PARAMOUNT PRESENTS
MAURICE CHEVALIER
IN
"LOVE ME TO-NIGHT"
WITH
JEANETTE MACDONALD
CHARLIE RUGGLES
CHARLES BUTTERWORTH
AND
MYRNA LOY
A ROUBEN MAMOULIAN PRODUCTION
BASED ON THE PLAY BY
LEOPOLD MARCHAND
& PAUL ARMONT
Famous Music
CORPORATION
MADE IN U.S.A.

MY LOVE PARADE
THE · LOVE · PARADE ·
· A PARAMOUNT MUSICAL ROMANCE ·
· WORDS · AND · MUSIC · BY ·
· VICTOR · SCHERTZINGER ·
AND
· CLIFFORD · GREY ·
Dream Lover
My Love Parade
FAMOUS MUSIC
CORPORATION

LIVIN' IN THE SUNLIGHT—LOVIN' IN THE MOONLIGHT
WORDS BY AL LEWIS
MUSIC BY AL SHERMAN
from the Paramount Picture "The Big Pond"
STARRING
MAURICE CHEVALIER
AND FEATURING
CLAUDETTE COLBERT
Famous Music

THE GAUCHE YEARS
(1888-1901)

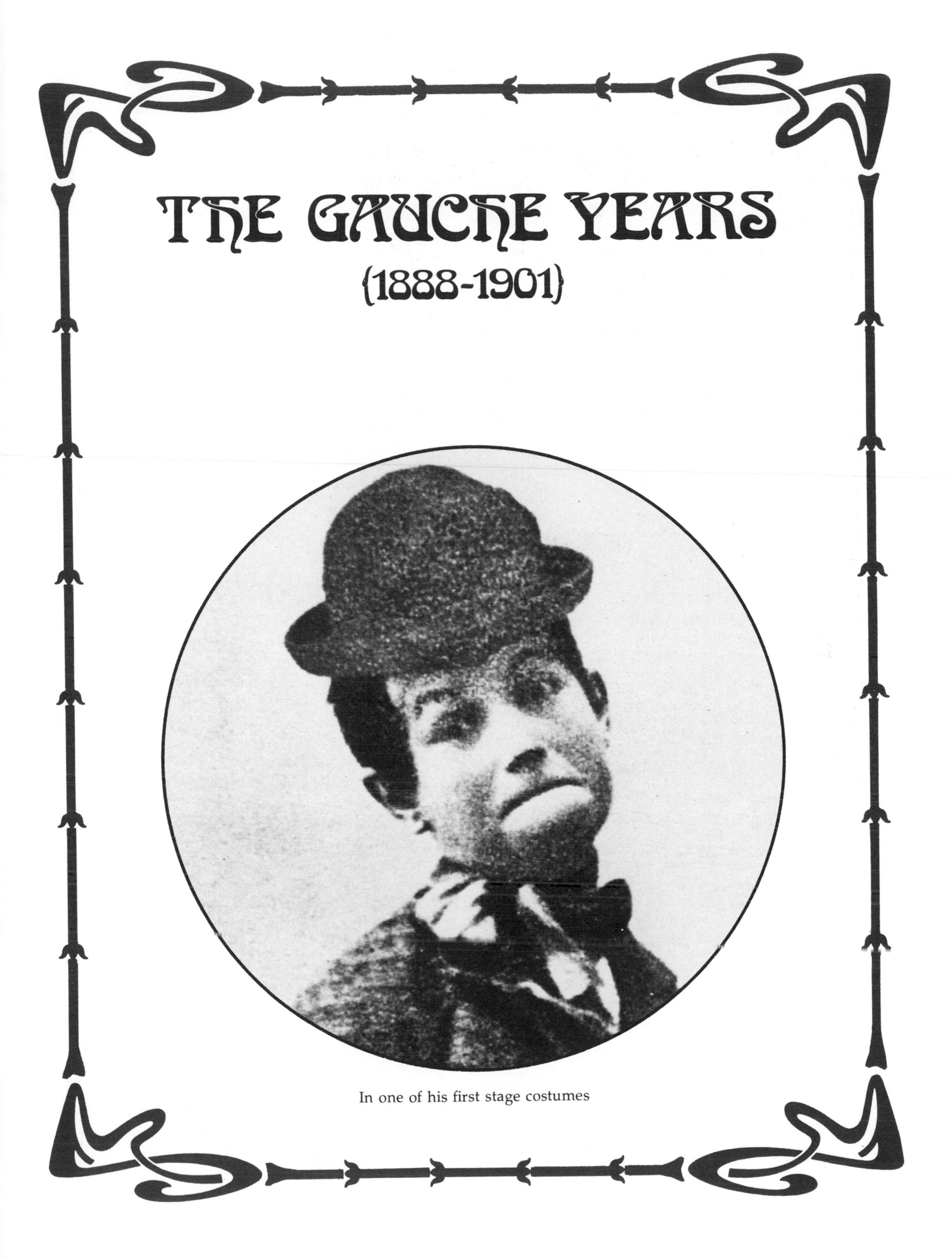

In one of his first stage costumes

If he had been born in England, where the great comedians are honored with titles, he would have become Sir Maurice. Here, he could lay claim to a title, a particular one worth much more than all the others. Here he was, and remains in the memory of all who knew him, "Maurice de Paris."

—RENÉ CLAIR, Paris, 1972

During the years immediately following the Franco-Prussian War, France was enshrouded with the ignominious memories of siege, occupation and defeat; and even her textbook maps of the lost provinces of Alsace-Lorraine were colored a deep purple—for mourning. It was during this dark time in her history when a very wise man said, "France is broken—but the pieces are still good."

It was not until 1888, however, when Frenchmen, still feeling their scars of shame and dishonor, found that in spite of all the anger, despair and hatred that was coiled inside them, a miraculous and truly remarkable national pride was being nurtured within their hearts. So much so that when "La Marseillaise" was played, all citizens rose in silence, uncovered their heads and stood at attention. This had not even occurred in the days of the Revolution when the inspired Rouget de l'Isle had composed the national anthem!

The Republic, aware of the awakened *esprit de corps* of her people, declared July 14 a national holiday that was to be celebrated each ,year in remembrance of the Fall of the Bastille, ninety-nine years earlier.

That year, 1888, in the city of Paris, soaring high over the rooftops on the Champ-de-Mars bordering the Seine, rose the Eiffel Tower, a structure being erected as part of the celebration of the Grand Exposition that was officially opening the following year. The Tower, intended as the symbol of the Exposition which anticipated the era of *La Belle Epoque*—The Gay Nineties—also seemed to be a monument that symbolized the new Paris and her dazzling society which, rising like a Phoenix from the ashes, was already dictating culture and style to the rest of the civilized world.

And in Paris, on the night of September 12, 1888, workers testing the electric circuits of the Eiffel Tower, lighted its structure for the first time. And in Ménilmontant, a suburban hillside village that was home to 90 percent of the poor workers of Paris, whose lives, nevertheless, were enriched by the pride they felt in helping the great city pulsate with a *joie de vivre* felt around the clock and around the world, the lighted Tower could be seen!

Earlier that same day in Ménilmontant, inside 29 rue du Retrait, a humble house situated on top of one of the hills, a boy—Maurice Auguste Chevalier—was born who was destined, like the Eiffel Tower, to become the symbol of twentieth-century Paris, just as Sarah Bernhardt had symbolized it during the last quarter of the nineteenth century.

The youngest of the three surviving sons born to Josephine and Victor Charles Chevalier, whose seven other children had not lived beyond infancy, Maurice was just a toddler when his parents, and brother Charles and brother Paul, moved to another part of Ménilmontant and were quartered in a small, two room apartment at 15 rue Julien Lacroix.

Josephine Chevalier, who had been born in Belgium, was a frail but industrious woman who rose in the morning with the first rays of sunlight, attended the needs of her family and home, and then in the evening, applied herself assiduously to her lace-making; a craft which earned her a few francs each week that were carefully hoarded for a family emergency, and which kept her busy until late at night when the kerosene lamp flickered and finally extinguished as the tongue of flame atop the coarsely woven wick consumed the last drops of the day's supply of oil.

Victor Charles Chevalier was a house painter who, when he wished to be, was industrious and adept at his trade. His oldest son Charles was his assistant and his middle son Paul was serving an apprenticeship as a metals engraver. When Maurice, the youngest son, whose head was then somewhat too large for his frail body, was six years old he was sent to *Ecole des Frères*, the free Catholic school. But just two years later, Victor, who was now a hopeless alcoholic, deserted his family after stumbling out of their apartment one night in a drunken stupor, and never returned.

Josephine and her sons stoically accepted his departure, and while they remained a family unit none of them ever spoke of him again. But each of them, with silent horror, remembered all the dreaded nights of drunken abuse, the mornings of painful silence, followed by contrite apologies and fervently passionate vows of abstinence which always preceded the eventual "all-I-need-is-just-one-drink-to-straighten-me-out" declaration which was immediately fulfilled and inexorably started the whole cycle over.

After the sudden but unlamented departure of his father, Charles become the reluctant head of the family. He worked diligently and struggled to

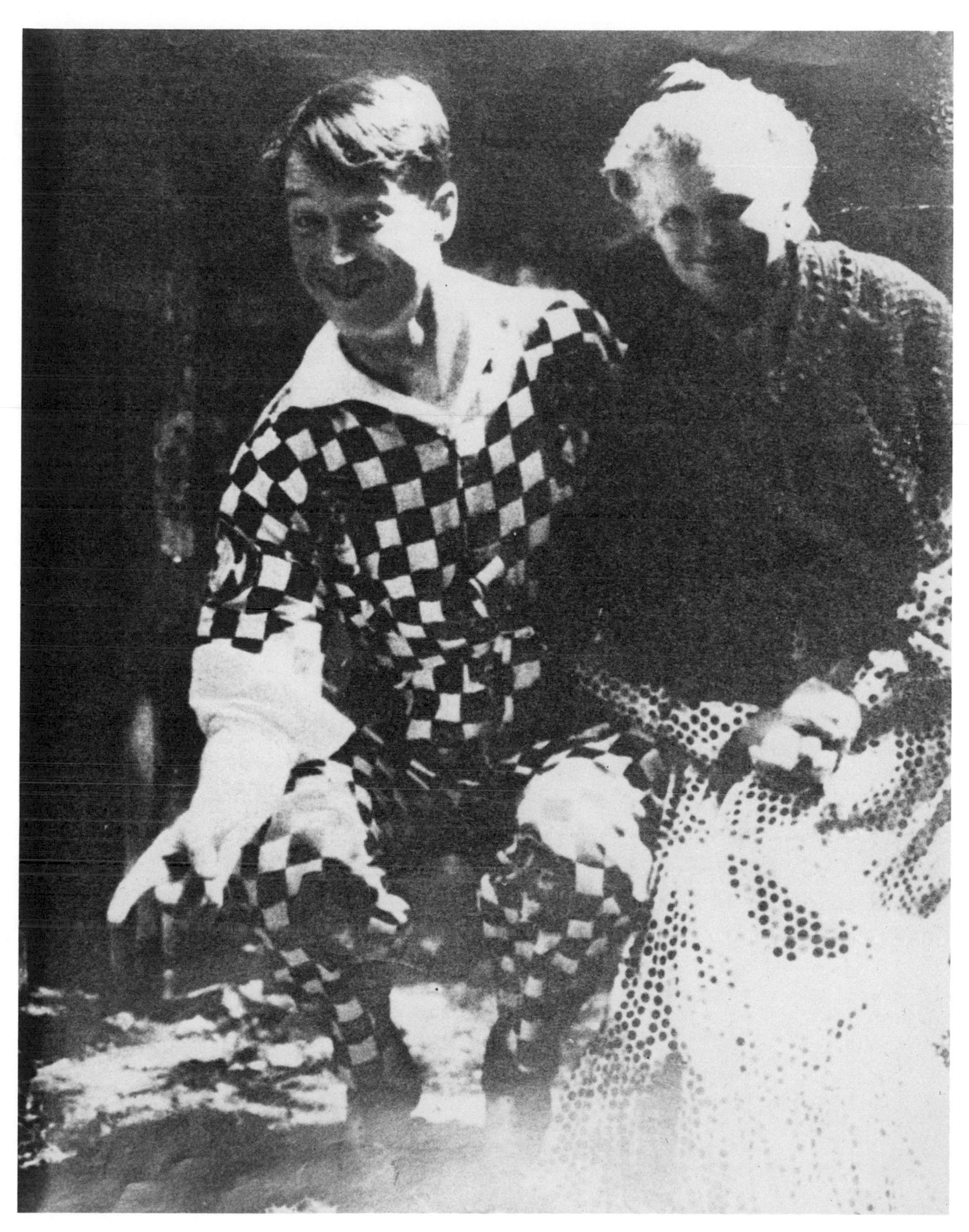

With his mother, affectionately called La Louque

keep the family together, although his heart was not in it. It belonged to the girl he wanted to marry and with whom he wished to establish his own domicile. Understanding this, Josephine convinced him he should follow the dictates of his heart. And so the burden of caring for his mother and young brother fell on Paul's shoulders. But he was not yet a fully accredited engraver and the three francs a day he earned was insufficient for the family to survive on. It was a bitter winter and nine-year-old Maurice, truant from school, worked all day with a snow removal crew to help out. Each night, muscles aching and sore and his feet wet and cold, he hurried home with a franc or two clutched in his blistered, frost-bitten hands which he joyously handed to his mother.

Many years later, while making *Can-Can,* he recalled the Christmas Eve of 1897, when he used some of the money earned helping to clear the streets and sewers to buy his mother a Christmas present. In typically practical French tradition, his gift was a loaf of freshly baked, oven-hot bread on which he warmed his hands as he hurried home with it through the snow.

"To this day," he said, "I can still smell the aroma of that bread. Surely it was the most delicious I have ever tasted! And *La Louque!* How I remember her smile as I handed it to her. When she bent down and kissed me, she looked at my raw hands and then gently rubbed some grease on them to soothe them. Later, while eating a piece of her 'Christmas present,' I licked the grease from my fingers. It was a banquet!"

Realizing that she could not forsake any of the short four years of education her son would get, and aware that he must not jeopardize getting his certificate of accomplishment which would legally permit him to work when he was ten years old, *La Louque*—the nickname of endearment by which her sons called Josephine Chevalier—went to work nights as a cleaning woman but, instead of resting during the day, she made lace that she sold for a few francs until her eyesight failed her and she collapsed from sheer exhaustion. For a while it was necessary for her to remain under a doctor's care in the charity ward of the Catholic hospital.

Unable to cope with things on his own, Paul was forced to send Maurice to the Alms House of the Children's Aid Society, located far across the city. A kind neighbor accompanied him on the trip which took him through the throbbing metropolis of Paris for the first time in his life. It was exciting, totally different from anything he had seen in Ménilmontant and he marvelled with the same wide-eyed wonderment a child from Brooklyn might then have registered when he had encountered Manhattan, "the Baghdad on the Hudson," for the first time.

He was well treated at the Alms House where he was given a navy blue uniform and a pair of high-topped black shoes to wear. Every night before saying his prayers and slipping into the hard-matted bed to which he had been assigned, he was required to polish those shoes until the inexpensive leather glowed with a high lustre. And he was given sufficient food to keep from being hungry, which he had often been after his father had deserted him. But, like all the other children there who had come from broken, poverty-stricken homes, he was abysmally homesick and for the first weeks he nightly cried himself to sleep. But he kept going, being toughened in the process, and living for the day when his mother, his beloved La Louque, would be well again and able to provide him with a home.

Then, one rainy afternoon, he was summoned to the office where the supervising priest told him the news: his mother had recovered, was able to provide him with a home, and would be coming for him the following Sunday! At their tearful reunion they greeted each other with shouts of joy and bursts of sudden laughter punctuated the excited accounts each gave the other simultaneously as they journeyed back to Ménilmontant.

And life for them all took a turn for the better. They were again living at 15 rue Julien Lacroix, now in a street level apartment, and Paul was a full-fledged engraver, earning a weekly forty-two francs! Maurice, now almost eleven, had completed the required four years of school and was given a job as an apprentice engraver at the foundry where his brother Paul was employed. So, at the end of his first full week of employment, he prevailed upon Paul and La Louque to accompany him to a performance of the Cirque Medrano, a third-rate circus performed in a Paris amphitheatre. Fascinated by the trapeze artists, Maurice announced after the performance that he wanted to be an acrobat. La Louque and Paul, remembering his fear of heights, laughed at his droll sense of humor. But the following week, after they attended a performance of the Cirque d'Hiver, Maurice's enthusiasm was more passionate than ever and he convinced his brother Paul to join him.

After that their attendance at performances of the Cirque became a weekend ritual and their evenings were spent at the Arras Gymnasium where they practiced and rehearsed some of the feats they had seen executed by the professionals they envied and hoped to be. But Maurice did not limit his ambitions and daydreams of "The Flying Chevaliers" to idle moments. Before too long the owners of the foundry where he and Paul worked were convinced he would never qualify as an engraver and he was fired for not having any interest in his work. Fearing the same fate might be in store for him, Paul told his young brother he was deserting the "act" and would remain where he was.

Surprised and disappointed, Maurice was far from discouraged in pursuing his ambition. All Paul's decision really meant was that somehow, somewhere, he would have to find another partner or become a soloist of the high wire. In any event, it was time for him to do something!

What he did was apply for a job with the Cirque d'Hiver where he was hired, at no salary, as a standby member of their acrobatic trio. As such he worked out with them every day and otherwise earned his keep by helping to clean up after the performances, selling refreshments and always silently praying that one member of the trio would be stricken with an ailment serious enough to prevent him from performing and he would be rushed in as his replacement. His prayer, however, went unanswered. One day while working out with the remarkably healthy trio, *he* fell from a high wire and was painfully injured.

Bedridden weeks with a fractured pelvis, he was forbidden by La Louque to work at the Cirque d'Hiver when he could walk again. Resigned that his acrobatic career had ended, almost before it began, Maurice, just as stagestruck as ever, was frustrated by his burning ambition to "make people forget their poverty and be happy" since there appeared to be no outlet for this inner drive. At thirteen, however, he had hardly explored all the possibilities of the entertainment world so, while he luxuriated in his daydreams, he labored as an apprentice carpenter, an electrician's helper, a penmaker and a paint mixer in a doll factory. From each job, however, he was fired—and always for the same reason: daydreaming and taking no interest whatever in what he was being paid to do.

The job he managed to keep the longest at this conjuncture was working in a nail factory as the operator of a manual punch press that turned out thumbtacks. It required a great exertion of energy and a minimum amount of concentration to operate

With La Louque

this machine so the arrangement seemed ideal. Unfortunately Maurice, in a moment of absent-mindedness, mashed his thumb in the mechanism. The accident caused the termination of his employment and the permanent disfigurement of his right thumb.

Once when someone asked if his hammer thumb was a discomfit and a liability, Chevalier smiled his famous smile and, with a wink, said, "No, not really. Although there have been occasions when I have been awkward—especially when I was in a hurry to unbutton an inviting bodice."

Paul, La Louque and Maurice occasionally went to the Café des Trois Lions on a Saturday night where they sipped cheap wine and watched the comics and singers hired to entertain the earthy denizens of Ménilmontant perform. Those who pleased the uninhibited crowd were applauded and cheered and those who did not please them were bombarded with overripe missives of vegetable origin. It was all done, on the part of spectator and performer, with great *bonhomie.* But a chance remark made by La Louque one night, a moment after she had been convulsed with laughter by a comic singer, "See *mon cheri,* that is what you should have done instead of trying to be a human fly. It would have been much safer!" started her young son thinking that it was not too late for him to be a music hall entertainer.

He had no voice, and no training whatever. And no idea how to go about accomplishing this new ambition. But he bought some sheet music and studied it. He rehearsed singing, without accompaniment, and talked La Louque, who was beginning to complain, into making him a costume. Then, one Saturday night the Chevalier trio arrived at the Café des Trois Lions and prevailed upon the impresario to give Maurice, resplendent in his just completed tramp costume, an audition. Since they were regulars at the cafe, and there was a slight chance the boy might have talent, the manager, taking no chances on offending his customers, agreed.

When Maurice's moment came, he nervously stumbled on stage amid cheers from his neighbors. In his ignorance and anxiety, he got off to a gauche beginning by singing three keys higher than the piano accompaniment. Realizing something was wrong, and having neither the presence or professionalism to correct it, he speeded up his singing and finished the song way ahead of the pianist. It was obvious to the audience and the accompanist that he was a rank amateur and the reaction all around was most derisive. La Louque remained his champion. "At least," she said, after he had slinked back to their table, "you didn't forget to smile."

After that catastrophe, whenever he encountered a neighbor who had witnessed or heard about it, they would point to him, laugh and catcall "Little

Blockhead." Instead of finding this a source of humiliation, Maurice reasoned he had been noticed and remembered. "All right," he told himself, "anyone could have been forgettably bad. But I was worse than that. Since there is but one way to go, I will try again and one day I will be a success."

As a teenager, Chevalier posed for a series of postcards.

THE GREEN YEARS
(1901-1918)

At the Casino de Paris

We will remember him singing in his own irresistible way songs which even if we didn't understand French, we would enjoy because we loved the way he sang them.
—HERMIONE GINGOLD.

A professional singer named Gilbert, who had occasionally appeared at the Café des Trois Lions, thought the Little Blockhead had guts and told him so on a day they chanced to meet. Gilbert also suggested that Maurice learn to sing with piano accompaniment before attempting another public appearance. That advice seemed like the financially insurmountable obstacle which would curtail another attempt at a career before it even started. But success is achieved by making possible the impossible. So, in exchange for some lace which La Louque agreed to make, a singing teacher agreed to teach him how to read music and to give him voice lessons.

A few weeks later Maurice approached the manager at the cafe of his fiasco to let him sing again. Marvelling that anyone could have such a monumental ego and such a minimal talent, the startled impresario agreed, thinking the ensuing spectacle would amuse his customers. Much to his surprise, however, he discovered Maurice was now singing three keys lower and that he managed to end the lyric simultaneously with the accompanist finishing the music! The audience was far from electrified but the sadistically hoped for spectacle of blood on the part of the manager was averted and Maurice was able to exit unmolested, if not exalted.

The singing lessons continued until the teacher's daughter had a complete selection of delicate lace in her trousseau. In the meantime Maurice haunted other Ménilmontant cafes begging for a chance to audition. His style and appeal improved with each appearance. His neighbors now regarded him less derisively and one day, after a woman stopped him on the boulevard to suggest a song he might sing at a future audition, he was elated.

Shortly after relating this incident to Gilbert, his *bon ami* arranged an audition for him at the Tourelles Casino on the Sunday evening before the Christmas of 1901. It went so well he was engaged at twelve francs a week, with a three francs a week bonus for rehearsals. That was two francs a week more than he had been making at the nail factory where his accident had terminated his employment a few days earlier. His sudden engagement meant Christmas would not be the bleak holiday he had anticipated. It also meant he was now a professional singer and a bona fide member of the entertainment world.

His euphoria, however, was short-lived. Because three weeks later the bill at the Tourelles Casino was changed and he found himself professionally at liberty. By scrounging around here and there at the cafes which dotted Paris he managed to get a week's booking at La Ville Japonaise, two weeks at the Casino de Montmartre and to "pick up a little time" at La Fourmi. When one of the other entertainers on a bill with whom he had worked before heard how long he had looked around before getting the engagement, he suggested Maurice acquire an agent and gave him the name of a man with a good reputation.

He finally persuaded this man, Dalos, to represent him. The association turned out to be one of mutual advantage because one of the agent's clients was the manager of the Concert de l'Univers, a rowdy music hall where most entertainers with any kind of following refused to appear for more than a week and never sought an encore engagement. Maurice had the stamina to remain *three months* and to develop a cult whose idea of entertainment was to circulate from cafe to cafe seeking and supporting the singers whose repertoires included the bawdiest songs. Retaining the tramp costume La Louque had made for him, and jauntily singing bawdy ballads—about milkmaids with bouncing bosoms; boulevardiers frustrated in their seduction attempts by unbelievable contretemps; the farmboy's first bordello encounter; or, its variation—a madame's first encounter with bucolic innocence—he was soon adored by the *paisants* and *bourgeois* who frequented the Montmartre honky tonks.

His success prompted Dalos to think he was ready for the provinces, so he arranged to send him on a tour that included engagements at Le Havre, Amiens and Tours. Upon his return he found that his brother Paul was about to be married. After the wedding he and La Louque moved to 118 Faubourg Saint-Martin into an apartment almost in the heart of the music and cafe world. A short period of idleness was followed by a week's engagement at the Petit Casino and the whole summer became a bohemian adventure where banquets and famines alternated their existence with more of the latter and less of the former as winter approached.

It was not until the following August, late in the summer of 1904, when Maurice was given a solo spot and featured in the ensemble of the revue *Satyre Bouchonné* which played at the Parisiana, the best of the boulevard music halls, that his fortunes, and his style, changed. Until that time his act had

The legendary Mistinguett

been a *pot-pourri* of songs, jokes, gestures and bits of business he had seen other performers use and had adopted. *Satyre Bouchonné* was a sophisticated entertainment in which his novelty solo was a pleasant interlude but it was not greeted with the enthusiasm of the ensemble songs, slyly suggestive in lyric and blatant in beat and melody, he helped perform. This was the first inkling he had that his material, far from *passé*, was, nonetheless, limited in appeal. Hoping to ameliorate his act, he became interested in knowing what other performers were accomplishing.

"My first influence," he later recalled, "was the American music hall. I remember seeing the Tiller Girls in Paris sing 'Yankee Doodle Dandy' with that crazy tempo. I went mad. What I did was to mix the American novelty and the old French humor so that even to the French I was something new."

During a three-week engagement at the Eden-Concert in Asnières, he introduced his new singing style, an easy-going, insinuating ebullience set to a staccato tempo to which audiences immediately responded, and which was to become synonymous with the Chevalier name. Resplendent in a striped jersey, with all hints of formality obscured by a dapper derby, worn at a rakish angle, and often used to emphasis a line of lyric, his popularity had Dalos arrange a tour. For the next six months he appeared in Brussels, Lille, Nice, Lyons, Bordeaux and Avignon winning audience approval and invitations from the management for return engagements. The climax of the tour was a smashing engagement at the Alcazar in Marseilles where, not yet nineteen years old, he was applauded by one of the theatrical legends of France—Sarah Bernhardt, who had made it a point to come and see him.

The news of his out-of-town triumphs preceded him back to Paris where the talk of the music halls was the "Chevalier Style" of singing which already had a dozen imitators. La Louque took great pride in being the mother of a celebrity. And for relaxation, Maurice worked out at the Arras Gymnasium where he and his brother Paul had once worked on their "acrobatic act" and where he took up boxing. It was there that he got to know Georges Carpentier, with whom he would one day work, and who would one day be an international star in the sport and theatrical worlds.

When he was asked to replace the very popular star Dranem who was suddenly taken ill, for an engagement at the Eldorado, one of the really chic bistros of Paris, Maurice felt he had really arrived. That triumph, however, was immediately overshadowed after P. L. Flers, producer of the Folies Bergère, saw him and was impressed. Enough to return the following evening for a dressing room conference which culminated with Flers offering him a contract to appear at the Folies for three consecutive seasons. Overwhelmed, Maurice accepted the offer with alacrity.

But the morning after his Folies debut, in *Le Figaro,* the leading newspaper of Paris, the entertainment editor wrote that he had not been impressed with the Chevalier voice, style or charm, about which he had heard so much, and he wondered how anyone with such an illusive talent had made it to the stage of the *crème de la crème* of showplaces. To Maurice, such aspersions seemed a personal rather than professional evaluation of his performance and he was intimidated and infuriated by it. Criticism of his singing had never annoyed him. In point of fact, he considered that a tribute to his charm, personality and comic abilities which were, in his mind, the real foundation of his image. He was always a performer who seemed to give everything he had effortlessly so that audiences were only aware that he was there solely for their pleasure. This was certainly the antithesis of his off-stage behavior when, between shows, he was introverted and retiring. But immediately after the bad notice in *Le Figaro,* he became more moody and somewhat sullen, retreating to his dressing room, where he quietly sipped cognac and ruminated. He was not mature enough, or professionally sure of himself, to accept criticism he didn't consider constructive.

Impresario Flers was even more displeased than his new star by this unjust review since the public liked him enough to make him a sellout attraction in spite of a critical adversary whose opinion usually carried a great deal of weight. And when P. L. Flers presented his next Folies revue, the spectacular *Grande Revue d'Hiver,* which was the most expensively costumed and lavishly staged entertainment in the history of the showplace, he co-starred Maurice Chevalier with Jane Marnac, the new dancing sensation. The show was received with wild enthusiasm which the entertainment editor of *Le Figaro* praised in general, reserving special compliments for Maurice Chevalier in particular.

Concurrent with his Folies contract, which left him with his summers free, he signed to appear for two of the hot months at the Ambassadeurs, the most chic warm-weather spot in the Champs-Elysées. For the other two months he toured the provinces.

It was in Lyons that he met Colette Willy, an actress with aspirations of becoming a writer, who some years later commemorated their brief and bitter-sweet romance when, internationally known as Colette, she admitted that a character named Cavaillon who appeared in one of her most popular novels, *Le Vagabond,* was modelled after Maurice.

But it was the "Queen of the Paris Night," and the idol and ideal of every Frenchman, the long-legged, legendary Mistinguett, who captured his heart. Sixteen years his senior and a show business phenomenon, beautiful and vivacious Mistinguett was the rage of Paris and the darling of France. When he was still a youngster, Maurice had seen her perform at the Eldorado and had afterwards gone to her dressing room and shyly conveyed his admiration of her sophisticated talent.

Something about that visit touched her and haunted her and she remembered him. In her autobiography, she wrote:

> I recognized him three or four years later in a little night club in Montmartre where he was doing a cabaret turn. I watched him work. It was a revelation. He put the song over as if he were humming it to himself for his own pleasure, with a rhythm and a sureness of touch that took my breath away. His get-up had to be seen to be believed: a blue and white striped sailor jersey, a skimpy jacket and a bowler hat, which he used to startling effect. I met him again when I was playing at the Variétés, where he often came. We used to pass each other on the stairs. He smiled and I smiled back. He called me plain Mistinguett and I called him Chevalier.
>
> When I took up my employ as mistress of ceremonies at the Folies Bergère, with the "girls," the "boys," the ostrich feathers and the inevitable staircase, I found, to my delight, that Maurice was also in the cast.

Chevalier was overwhelmed to find himself working with the celebrated Mistinguett and surprised when he discovered she remembered his backstage visit. Their speciality number, a comedy skit which they later filmed *(La Valse Reversante),* was a burlesque of the ever popular Apache dance.

Chevalier headlined a show at the Folies-Bergère which also featured the Dolly Sisters.

And because they had to knock over furniture and generally perform with unusual zest, the number was intricate and the complicated choreography required an unusual number of rehearsals. Their formal backstage attitude dissolved before opening night. A sly wink led to a stolen kiss and a secret rendezvous climaxed with a night of delirious love-making. Their ten-year romance was as notable for the improbability of the protagonists, a chic, sophisticated older woman wise in the ways of romance and a virtually inexperienced younger man, as it was for the stormy clashes of temperament and the interludes of oblivious passion.

Their discreet "arrangement" seemed ideal. Maurice remained at home, arriving in the afternoon in time for a siesta before having dinner with La Louque and leaving for the theatre. Then, after the performance, he and Mistinguett, often accompanied by an entourage of dancing gypsies (chorus members), toured the Montmartre clubs and parted the following day after lunch at the Guillaume Tell, a small cafe on the Boulevard de Strasbourg. Only Maurice and Mistinguett seemed unaware that everyone in Paris knew their schedule.

It was 1908 when Chevalier had first worked in the movies, as an extra in a short-reel comedy,

In one of his early solo appearances when he toured the French provinces

Trop Crédule, directed by Jean Durand. But he was unimpressed with the silent cinema and logically concluded he had little to offer the medium. By 1912, however, he had worked in some Max Linder comedies and with Mistinguett.

"Those films were nothing," said Chevalier in July, 1959, when queried about them. "I was a straight man for Max Linder or just a partner for Mist—they were always the stars. My film career began here," he said, pointing down toward the floor of his dressing room to indicate he meant Hollywood. "If you put all my scenes together from those silent films I doubt that you would have more than thirty or thirty-five minutes of film."

In 1913, after postponing his required military service for five years, Chevalier joined the 35th Infantry in Belfort and started his two year tenure. He became friendly with another inductee, Maurice Yvain, a pianist and composer. They worked up an act which they performed at benefits. Mistinguett helped them keep the act *au courant* by sending him all the latest sheet music for the hit songs. But war was soon declared and the Germans invaded France. During his first encounter in enemy action, Chevalier was wounded and taken prisoner. Part of a bullet was taken from the back of his right lung in a Red Cross hospital and when he recuperated he was shipped to Alten Grabow, a prisoner-of-war camp in Germany. He remained there twenty-six months. In 1917, for his "valorous conduct" in battle three years earlier, he was awarded the Croix de Guerre.

While a prisoner, Chevalier had relieved the monotony by getting permission to build a stage at the rear of one of the barracks. There, with the help of other Parisians with show business backgrounds, he staged shows for the prisoners and the officers in charge of the installation. And there was always a weekly package—music, food, books—from either Mistinguett or La Louque who, during his absence, had become good friends.

When he was returned to France, via Geneva, Switzerland, as part of a prisoner exchange, Mistinguett and La Louque were there to meet him at the depot in Paris. Both were shocked to see how thin he had become and each did her best to pamper and indulge him during his first few days of freedom.

Late in 1916, he returned to the Folies Bergère as Mistinguett's dancing partner and soon after that, all dressed in white, they created a sensation at the Cigale dancing to "Broken Doll," an American jazz tune. Then, when the Armistice came, they took over a revue, *Laissez les Tomber*, from its stars, Gaby Deslys and Harry Pilcer, which was doing big business at the Casino de Paris. The arrangement seemed ideal until Chevalier demanded equal billing and Mistinguett refused it to him.

"And then," Mistinguett said, "the trouble started. Our success had no doubt gone to Maurice's head a bit, and he probably thought I was trying to sabotage his future. He stopped calling for me at the end of the performance, as he had done every night without fail for years."

"In spite of her sincere love," said Chevalier, "Mist always considered me just a foil for her great talent. She never thought of me as an equal on the stage, or as a rival. This saddened me as I could see no solution to the problem. I loved Mist, but I adored my profession and my independence."

Soon after that a solution to his professional and romantic problems presented itself in the person of Elsie Janis, the American star who was once described as "the most independent woman in show business."

Wearing the Croix de Guerre

With his comrades at Camp Alten Grabow in Germany where they were interned during World War I

At the Casino de Paris (1924)

THE GREAT YEARS
(1919-1939)

With a group of Wampus Baby Stars for 1931

Maurice Chevalier: The master of the most difficult and hazardous branch of the theatrical profession.

—MARLENE DIETRICH.

Soon after her introduction to Maurice Chevalier, Elsie Janis suggested he come to London and co-star with her in a revue. Flattered with the offer, he declined saying his English was not too good and he could not hope to compete with a British performer. Miss Janis laughed and disagreed, saying he had something no Englishman had ever possessed: Gallic charm. But early in 1919 when Owen Nares, Miss Janis' leading man in her revue, *Hullo, America,* which had opened late the previous year, announced he was leaving the show, Chevalier cabled her asking if her offer was still good. Her producer, Sir Alfred Butt, who also owned the Palace Theatre in Paris, immediately cabled back an affirmation.

His departure for London marked the beginning of the end of his romance with Mistinguett. But it had certainly been a tender, tempestuous and traumatic relationship and Chevalier was, perhaps, the one to profit the most from it. Mistinguett gave him self-assurance, and taught him that romantic and theatrical *savoir-faire* were essential to success. But it was Elsie Janis who taught him how to fuse his talents and his personality and refine them into stardom.

Miss Janis never doubted his potential and she worked with him, night and day, until every inflection and intonation of his songs was exactly right. And after he stepped before a British audience for the first time, and sang Cole Porter's "On the Level, You're a Little Devil," Miss Janis' belief in his potential was confirmed by the public and the press. But English audiences are seldom as excitable and demonstrative as the French, and Chevalier could not believe he was a success. When his three month contract ended, he only renewed after Sir Alfred agreed to let him appear in a French edition of *Hullo, America,* which he opened at his Palace Theatre in Paris, where it closed in record time.

Unconvinced he could succeed in a book show, Chevalier rejected a role in a musical comedy and returned to the Casino de Paris. In addition to a solo spot that allowed him to sing ten songs, he also bowed to the power of box-office nostalgia by agreeing to dance one number with Mistinguett. Her new partner Earl Leslie, a handsome American, was rumored to have replaced him in her affections. As if such a situation wasn't enough to generate backstage tensions around the Casino, Chevalier demanded, and got, equal billing. Psychologically unable to accept this, Mistinguett signed a contract to star, solo, in a production of *Madame Sans Gêne* going into immediate rehearsal. This left the whole marquee of the Casino for advertising Maurice Chevalier's nightly appearances.

In accordance with his star stature, he revised his act and, for the first time, appeared on stage wearing a tuxedo *and* a straw hat. The effect, lighthearted and elegant, was accepted immediately by the public—and the international admiration for the Chevalier image, a charming smile, a saucy song, an insouciant air and a straw hat, became a show business institution lasting more than forty years. If not the originator of the one-man show, he became its all-time standard bearer.

Instant stardom, after eighteen years in show business, brought him all sorts of lucrative offers. He rejected a chance to come to the U.S. to appear in a silent film and he turned down a concert tour of the English provinces. But he accepted the lead in a delightful operetta, *Dédé,* which opened at the Bouffes Parisiens and played there, to capacity, for two years. *Dédé* was *the* show for American visitors to see and they all took home more than enthusiastic reports about Maurice Chevalier, the toast of Paris. Among the more notable Americans to applaud him were Mary Pickford and Douglas Fairbanks. They came backstage to congratulate him and remained long enough to have their offer to finance a Broadway production of *Dédé,* with him as star, rejected. Miss Pickford and Fairbanks were well known for many things, and included was their steadfast rule of never taking "no" for an answer when they wished it to be otherwise.

So, a few nights later, they returned to Chevalier's dressing room with Charles Dillingham, who offered him an even more financially fantastic deal to bring *Dédé* to New York. Realizing there was no way he could lose, and he had everything to gain, he accepted Dillingham's offer once he carefully alerted him to the fact that *Dédé* would still run at least another year in Paris.

In order to best prepare for his U.S. stage debut, Chevalier decided a visit to New York during his eight-week summer vacation would be of tremendous help. When he confided his plan to Mistinguett she was elated. So much so that she decided to accompany him—and that Earl Leslie would accompany her. And so a rather reflective *ménage à trois* sailed for America.

Leslie, a New Yorker, planned dawn to dusk excursions of Manhattan for his French com-

With William S. Hart in 1929, being taught how to handle a six-shooter

Advertisement for his one-man show in 1931

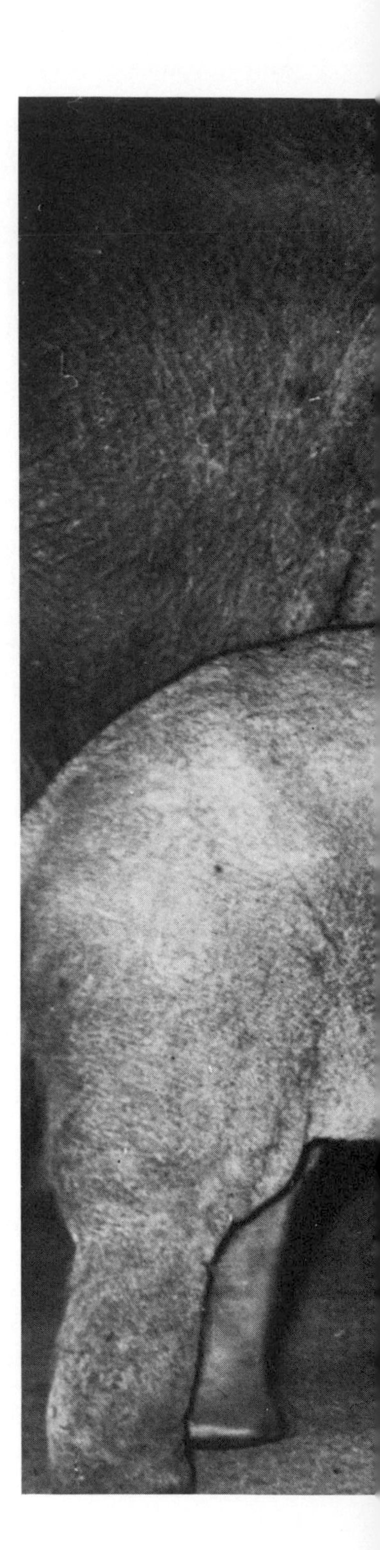

With Josephine Baker at the Cirque Medrano in 1937

With Douglas Fairbanks and Sir Harry Lauder in Hollywood, 1928.

panions; Mistinguett anticipated midnight to dawn revels at all the places she had been hearing about in whispers for years; and, Chevalier, the practical trio member, planned only to see the shows, listen to the latest songs, and take a few dance lessons.

So while Earl Leslie deferred his plans in order to escort Mistinguett, Chevalier learned all the latest jazz tunes and dances. The highlight of his visit, he later said, was seeing the sexually dynamic Josephine Baker in *Shuffle Along*. Many trepidations he had had about bringing *Dédé* to Broadway dispelled while he was there and he started the return trip thinking he and the show could be very successful.

But it turned out that he had little time for such pleasant daydreams—by the time they passed the Ambrose Lightship, the travelling trio was enmeshed in jealous arguments and fiery temperament flareups. It all started when Mistinguett complained because she had not received an offer to appear on Broadway comparable to what Dillingham had assured Chevalier he would receive. And when she ran out of argumentive ammunition, she sulked in her cabin. Earl Leslie did what he could to comfort her and Chevalier did what he could to avoid her (which turned out to be spending the entire voyage in one of the ship's lounges consuming cognac). When they reached Southampton, Mistinguett and Leslie debarked without a goodbye. Chevalier stood at the rail and watched her go—realizing that whatever feelings he had had for her were best remembered far away from her. He stayed on board the ship, crossed the English Channel, and debarked at Le Havre. In later years he never failed to acknowledge that she had been the great love of his life.

When someone once read her part of an interview in which he was quoted as saying this, Mistinguett smiled and nodded. "I may have forgotten the tenderness a little, but I have not forgotten Maurice Chevalier either," she said.

"Whenever I think of him I have the same tightening of my heartstrings as I do when I hear a bird sing." She paused a moment, took a delicate sip of her liqueur, and then added, "But birds sing in tune—that is their great secret."

Chevalier re-opened *Dédé* and as its second year's run commenced he began spending his after-theatre hours in the company of beautiful showgirls and his days working in some three-reel comedies, directed by Henri Diamant-Berger, who said:

"Maurice was rather silent and serious minded. As he was working on stage at night, and very

With Marlene Dietrich in 1932 after one of their "identically dressed" appearances

With chorus, in operetta *Dede*

careful about his health, he always went back to his dressing room when he was not shooting to get some rest." It was only much later, after he had completed a new film version of *Par Habitude*, that Diamant-Berger and everyone else realized he was mentally and physically exhausted and was drinking heavily.

His collapse and stay at a sanitarium to dry out surprised no one. But when he returned to work and paid to have a prompter on hand at each performance, everyone realized that his absolute dread of parting with a sou was minimized by his fear of going blank on stage. This could only mean that he, too, knew what others already suspected: his mental condition was unsound. Nevertheless, when *Dédé* closed with three months left to the season, he contracted to star in a new operetta, *Là-Haut*, which he thought would only be adequate enough to last until it was time to leave for New York. The rehearsals of *Là-Haut* were sheer agony for him but somehow he managed to get through them. Opening night was even more of an ordeal but, miraculously, the show turned out to be an enormous hit. Electing to remain with it, he arranged to buy his way out of his contract with Dillingham.

Paris was enchanted with his new show and he was considered to be "sitting on top of the world" although he had confided to one of the chorus girls with whom he danced a specialty number, Yvonne Vallée, that he was suffering from nervous exhaustion and on the verge of collapse. His breakdown was not long in coming and during the four months of his recovery at Saujon, Miss Vallée remained close by. Gossip soon filtered back to him that all Paris knew of his alcoholic problem, which was real enough, but the rumors that he was also suffering from satyriasis and the after effects of cocaine addiction infuriated him.

To squelch all talk that "he would never work again," he broke in a new act, with Yvonne Vallée as his dancing partner, at the provincial variety houses. The old magic still worked and audiences adored them. They were also aware that Chevalier knew of the gossip going around about him because one of the numbers he did with Miss Vallée was a parody of the famous Gallagher and Shean routine, patterned to fit his current situation:

"Et c'est vrai, M'sieu Chevalier?"
"Absolument, Mam'zelle Vallée!"

He established a box-office attendance record in the French theatre that for years remained unequalled, when he opened at the splendorous

The portrait which advertised his appearance in Ziegfeld's *Midnight Frolic*

With Jeanette MacDonald, between scenes of *One Hour with You*, 1932

Visiting Marlene Dietrich between scenes of her film *Song of Songs*, 1933

With his wife Yvonne at their home in France

With Marlene Dietrich on the set of *Love Me Tonight*

new Empire Theatre in Paris after his conquest of the provinces. The talk of his sensational new act, his beautiful new dancing partner and the condition of his health all helped to account for his remarkable resurgence. And when he returned to headline the show at the Casino de Paris, he had two numbers with Yvonne Vallée and two big production numbers with the fabulous Dolly Sisters. It was during this engagement that he introduced "Valentine," the first of the many songs which were to become part of his international repertoire. "I suppose," he ruminated many years later, "that I have sung 'Valentine' about ten thousand times!"

Early in 1927, Yvonne Vallée, who had put off Chevalier's proposals of marriage, finally acquiesced and became his wife. They were married in a civil ceremony by the mayor of Vaucresson, where Chevalier had rented a villa he named "Quand on est Deux," after one of his songs, and to where he and Miss Vallée had often retreated. They later repeated their marriage vows in a Catholic ceremony. Chevalier then purchased a "farm," an acre and a half of land and an old house he had remodeled, at La Boca, near Cannes, which he named "La Louque" and where his mother, for whom it had been named, lived for the remainder of her life.

On Irving Berlin's thirty-ninth birthday, May 11, 1927, which is also the date on which the Academy of Motion Picture Arts and Sciences was founded, The Chevaliers opened in London in a new revue, *White Birds,* which closed almost immediately afterward. Chevalier and Miss Vallée, who was pregnant, spent the summer enjoying themselves and making small jokes about their first failure as they faced the happy prospects of parenthood. But their son, born later that year, died at birth. Miss Vallée remained bedridden for several months after the tragedy.

Chevalier lost his grief by working in a new show at the Casino de Paris in which, for the benefit of the hundreds of rich American tourists who came nightly to cheer and applaud him, he did three numbers in English.

One especially crowded and boisterous night, early in 1928, Irving Thalberg, MGM's youthful executive producer, and his bride, Norma Shearer, came backstage to compliment him on the show and to invite him to take a screen test. Unaware that Thalberg had meant a sound test but still having no idea who he was, Chevalier declined and quickly got rid of them by pleading a headache and begging to be excused. But a moment after

Returning from Paris in 1930 with his wife

they had gone, his secretary, Max Ruppa, who had been unable to attract his attention while he was committing his big *gaffe,* explained who they were. He immediately sent after them with an apology and an invitation for them to join him for a midnight supper.

The sound test he made at the Vincennes studio enchanted Thalberg and Miss Shearer. Always severely critical of his own work, Chevalier was also very pleased with it. But when their discussion of a contract and terms reached an impasse, all he ended up getting from Thalberg was a print of his test which, it turned out, was all he needed.

That was because Jesse Lasky came backstage to see him two weeks later and he offered him a screen test. Chevalier groaned silently, wondering who Lasky was, and then he casually mentioned the test he just done. But instead of getting rid of his visitor by pleading a headache, he told him he could arrange for him to see the test. When the appointed time came, Chevalier, who had by now been "clued in" on the fact that Jesse Lasky *was* Paramount Pictures, arrived for the screening exuding charm.

The test, the charm, the talent—whatever—all pleased Lasky and he offered Chevalier an all-expenses paid contract which would pay him a fantastic salary for coming to Hollywood and working six weeks making a feature film. The offer was accepted without hesitation.

"I was very pleased with Lasky's frankness and his offer," Chevalier remarked afterward. "It was so practical! If I was a success I could bargain a much better contract than if I had insisted on signing one before making a film. And if I was a failure, well, neither of us would have to get ulcers wondering how we could get out of a bad bargain."

The U.S. trade papers made much of Chevalier signing with Lasky for a film. Ever since he had rejected playing a role in Mary Pickford's comedy, *Rosita,* which was Ernst Lubitsch's first American-made film, Chevalier's refusal of all U.S. film offers had been reported. Douglas Fairbanks had wanted him for a role in *The Iron Mask* and one of his greatest Hollywood admirers, George Fitzmaurice, had offered him roles in numerous films he directed.

"I'm glad I never accepted any of those offers," Chevalier said. "I was doing very well in Paris on the stage and I could see no logic in giving up that status to make Hollywood films as a supporting player in a silent feature. I do regret, of course, that I never made a film with my good friend Douglas Fairbanks. But perhaps we would not have been such good friends if I had played a small part in *The Iron Mask.*"

The Chevaliers sailed from France aboard the *Ile de France* and they arrived in New York on the evening of October 16, 1928. Director Robert Florey, a native of France, was then working at Paramount's Astoria studios on Long Island, and he was on hand to meet them. He had also been induced by Paramount executives to talk Chevalier into making a short film of his reactions to New York during the four days he would be there before entraining for Hollywood. Since the film was intended only for European theatres, Chevalier agreed. It was shot in three afternoons and one evening and called *Bonjour New York!*

On the eve of his departure for California, Chevalier sang "Valentine" to Jesse Lasky, Adolph Zukor, other Paramount executives and their wives, and a gathering of theatre owners at a supper-dance given in his honor at the Ritz-Carlton Hotel. Everyone present had good cause for rejoicing the anticipated celluloid success of their Gallic guest, because that was the era when authentic cowboys who could ride 'n' rope were replaced in movies by drugstore cowboys with guitars, who could play 'n' sing; when ingenues, whose entire careers had consisted of giggles and groans on a casting couch, found themselves replacing silent screen sirens who, in one recorded screech, went from stardom to oblivion; when, seemingly overnight, the studio sound stages became arenas of organized confusion as sound engineers, voice coaches and song writers collided with cameramen, directors and performers, all tripping over cables and dialog sequences as the movies stopped moving and the talkies began talking.

It was the same story at each studio until in October of 1928 when Maurice Chevalier arrived in Hollywood and reported for work at Paramount. Then, as filming commenced on *Innocents of Paris,* and the Frenchman protruded his lower lip in a scowl of amusement, spoke English with a delightful accent and sang, sometimes off-key, with his captivating style and distinctly charming manner, and cameras and recording equipment preserved on sound film the image that was Chevalier, the audible screen no longer seemed the ogre threatening everybody's security. It was suddenly obvious the moment of the sound film had indeed arrived and so had Chevalier—in time to be the screen's first talking superstar.

With La Louque and Yvonne Vallee in church, just after their wedding

Paramount executives screened the daily rushes of *Innocents of Paris* and enthusiastically started making deals for its first-run playdates with theatre exhibitors the third week it was in production. Before the end of the fourth week, Chevalier was offered a year's extension on his short-term contract at a fabulous salary that guaranteed him over half a million dollars. Loathing the script, and very displeased because Harry d'Abbadie d'Arrast, who had made several delightful films he admired, had rejected directing the film (and had been replaced by Richard Wallace), Chevalier accepted the offer at once, positive the film would be a disaster and Paramount would pay him off rather than make a subsequent film with him.

He confided these fears to his good friend Douglas Fairbanks, with whom he played tennis most weekends and, occasionally, doubles with Charlie Chaplin and Fairbanks' daughter-in-law, Joan Crawford. Well aware that Chevalier's doubts were groundless, Fairbanks gave up trying to convince him, knowing the release of his film and its reception would elate his French friend. But Richard Wallace and his wife, with whom Chevalier and his wife Yvonne Vallée attended whatever sporting event was being presented in or around Hollywood, were always ready to boost his spirits.

Through it all, Yvonne Vallée seldom left her husband's side. Unobtrusive, but ever watchful, she was present at the studio each day, content to remain on the sidelines and watch the filming. She was unreceptive to all overtures of friendship made by the wives of various executives who tried to include her in their plans for afternoon bridge games and shopping sprees. Talented and ambitious when she first met Chevalier, she no longer had any interest in a career of her own. Somewhat vehemently, she declined all proposals to act in the French-language versions of films then being made simultaneous with English-language ones at all studios. Paramount, Fox and MGM had all come forward with attractive offers.

The press and public reception to *Innocents of Paris* surpassed all of Paramount's expectations.

Everywhere, everyone was humming a new song, "Louise," introduced by a new film star, Chevalier, whose fears of failure were allayed—briefly. When Paramount announced he would next romance Jeanette MacDonald while impersonating a suave, debonaire officer in the army of a mythical kingdom in an operetta called *The Love Parade,* to be directed by Ernst Lubitsch, Chevalier was quick to remind everyone he was past 40.

When he heard that, Lubitsch said, "In that case he should stop acting like a twenty-year-old prima donna!" Lubitsch also insisted on having gallery portraits made of Chevalier in his costumes and having him rehearse all the songs he would be singing. And, because the script was incomplete, he also suggested Chevalier attend all story conferences and he instructed his writers to listen to any ideas he had. In a short time, Chevalier was waxing more enthusiastic than anyone else over *The Love Parade* and collecting an astronomical salary while waiting for filming to begin.

Much to Paramount's pleasure, Florenz Ziegfeld, Jr. offered to star Chevalier on Broadway in his late-night to dawn show, *Midnight Frolic,* which was being presented at the New Amsterdam Roof in New York City, during the interim when the script of *The Love Parade* would be completed and filming would commence. Backed by Paul Whiteman's orchestra, Chevalier headlined a show that included as co-stars Helen Morgan and the Duncan Sisters. It played to capacity audiences for six weeks

With his wife and Adolphe Menjou in 1928

Arriving with his wife in New York in 1931

With his wife, 1931

starting in early February, 1929. And while he was making his U.S. stage debut, *Innocents of Paris* was the current hit movie.

After he returned to Hollywood and filmed *The Love Parade,* he remained long enough to film his three sequences which were part of the footage of the all-star musical revue *Paramount on Parade* before returning in triumph to France. At the Paris depot he was mobbed by hordes of women waving placards, strewing flowers in his wake and shouting "Vive Maurice!" When he told his mother about this reception, La Louque smiled, patted his cheek and said, "It's no more than you deserve, my son."

In conjunction with the openings of both *Bonjour New York!* and *Innocents of Paris* in the cinemas, Chevalier played a special six-week engagement at the Empire Theatre which had over one hundred standees at every performance! Back in Hollywood, Ernst Lubitsch rushed ecstatically from a preview showing of *The Love Parade,* his first sound film, to send him a cable: "You are sitting on top of the world, Maurice!"

And indeed he was—for a while. His new contract with Paramount guaranteed him $20,000 a week plus round-trip traveling expenses for him and his wife to France, twice a year. Under this new agreement, he filmed *The Big Pond* in English- and French-language versions, with Claudette Colbert as his leading lady in both productions, at Paramount's Astoria studio on Long Island.

When he returned to Hollywood to make a film, *Playboy of Paris,* which was a project close to his heart, he learned he had been nominated for an Academy Award for his performances in *The Love Parade* and *The Big Pond,* which added to his high spirits. Originally *Playboy of Paris* had been a silent Max Linder comedy, *Le Petit Café,* which Chevalier had hoped would have been remade as a sound feature for his first U.S. film. Paramount made *Playboy of Paris* in English- and French-language versions *(Le Petit Café);* in the former, Frances Dee was the ingenue; in the latter, Chevalier's wife Yvonne Vallée played the part. It was the only film she ever made in the U.S. While these were in production, Marlene Dietrich became a constant set visitor. An easy camaraderie developed between Miss Dietrich and Chevalier, the kind of relationship she shared with several internationally well-known men, but it was, nevertheless, a relationship that Miss Vallée distrusted.

After the two versions of *Playboy of Paris* were completed, the no longer harmoniously married Chevaliers returned to Paris where he opened in a revue at the Casino de Paris, without a girl partner. Because his mother was in frail condition and her health was not good, he postponed his U.S. return an additional four weeks. But when she rallied and seemed to be in better health, he returned to New York to film *The Smiling Lieutenant.* The return voyage was an ordeal and he sent La Louque daily cablegrams in an effort to cheer her ebbing spirits. But on the first day of filming, the news came from Paris that she had died.

Disconsolate, Chevalier insisted on working although he collapsed in sorrow in his dressing room after each take was filmed. And since it was being filmed in two versions, English and French, it was an extraordinarily long filming schedule.

Said director Ernst Lubitsch, "I was busy on the set but out of the corner of my eye I would see him sitting quietly in a corner; grave and serious. He never talked much or laughed with any of the others.

"Then when I was ready to shoot a scene—before us, in a split second, is the same man. The same man? No, a very different man, a man of force and sparkle, a very dynamo of a man, whose underlip sticks out, and whose irresistible personality has captivated millions of men and women all over the world."

The Chevaliers returned to Hollywood and he made *One Hour with You* before they returned to France. There, between daily visits to St. Vincent's Cemetery in Paris where he mourned and prayed before his mother's grave, he made a two-reel Spanish language film, *El Cliente Seductor,* at the Pathé studios at Joinville which Paramount had taken over. It's a curious Chevalier film credit which apparently has never had distribution in English-speaking countries. Miss Vallée underwent surgery for a feminine disorder during this trip and was not strong enough to accompany her husband when the time came for him to return to Hollywood.

Newspaper columnists were quick to note Chevalier's solo status (when he had first arrived in Hollywood to make *Innocents of Paris,* one magazine writer likened his bringing his wife along to "Taking an old ham sandwich to a banquet") and to report to their readers that almost nightly his dinner companion was Marlene Dietrich. Once this was reported in the Paris newspapers, Miss Vallée wasted no time in returning to Hollywood to face her husband acrimoniously.

Said Chevalier, "Certain words should never be said between two people, for they are too cruel ever to be erased and you can never buy them back. We spoke such words to each other. And once we had done so our marriage was ended forever. I consulted my attorneys and I instructed them to give her anything she wanted." He paused a moment and sighed. "I never got married again. Several times I was tempted, yes, this is true, but each time my head, not my heart, did the reasoning. Since that was the case perhaps it is just as well . . ."

After obtaining her divorce in Paris, Miss Vallée, except for rare encounters, faded from Chevalier's life, always refusing offers to publish the story of her marriage. Visibly fighting tears, she was, however, among the multitude of mourners who attended his funeral some forty years later.

While suffering the after-shock of his mother's death and the disintegration of his marriage, Chevalier worked at making his best film, Rouben Mamoulian's exquisite musical *Love Me Tonight*. Once free, however, a new social life opened up for him in Hollywood.

Fellow countryman and good friend Charles Boyer opened up the world of literature to Chevalier, and he began reading all the great French classics he had merely heard about. Soon the essays of Montaigne became his daily inspiration. And his nightly inspiration was in the dark and exotic beauty of Kay Francis with whom he was constantly seen. Rumor had it that they were in love and would marry, although Miss Francis maintained otherwise. Her interests, it turned out, were neither in her career nor another marriage and eventually her esoteric life revolved solely around herself and whatever aspiring ingenue was her current protégée.

Of Chevalier's romance with Miss Francis and its eventual termination, Robert Florey recalls:

"When all was going well in his love affair he could be very gay; he would dance around and hum Schertzinger tunes or some of his early songs. But then, when he was unhappy, I would find him despondent and talking about returning to Paris immediately. Charles Boyer has told me he used to witness the same kind of emotional outbursts."

Having reached his cinematic apex in the 1930's with *Love Me Tonight*, Chevalier's film career in Hollywood for the next few years vacillated from two indifferent comedies, *A Bedtime Story* and *The Way to Love*, that ended his Paramount tenure, to MGM's visually handsome and very popular new version of *The Merry Widow*, and to Roy Del Ruth's wickedly

With director Rene Clair on the set of *Le Silence est d'Or*

amusing and tunefully staged musical *Folies Bergère*. That was Chevalier's last U.S. made film before World War II. It was twenty-two years before he made another film in Hollywood.

It happened that he didn't renew his Paramount contract after completing *The Way to Love;* instead, he signed a lucrative one with MGM that promised him life-time security. But after co-starring with Jeanette MacDonald in one film *(The Merry Widow)* and refusing to take second billing to Grace Moore in another *(The Chocolate Soldier)* that agreement, by mutual consent, was terminated. That professional impasse was a repeat of a situation he had encountered some years earlier with Mistinguett at the Casino de Paris, only now the roles were reversed!

Of the last film he made in Hollywood during the 1930's, *Folies Bergère,* Chevalier has said:

"I liked it very much, especially the French version. It's one of my best films. Originally my good friend Charles Boyer was asked to make it. He refused and suggested that I do it. A few years later I was offered a musical version of *Pepe Le Moko* which I suggested Boyer do. He did sing in the U.S. film version, which was called *Algiers,* but it was just a dramatic new version. The musical version *(Casbah)* was not made until years later, after the war, and by then I was too old for it."

When asked about Jeanette MacDonald, his four-time co-star, when he was making *I'd Rather Be Rich* (1964), Chevalier confided:

> She is a very sweet and very talented girl, about twelve years younger than I am, although she always professed to being even younger than that. At the time we worked together she was very much in love with Bob Ritchie. But he, of course, was not the man for her. Their marriage, or arrangement—although I'm sure they were married, otherwise it's difficult to understand why she allowed him to mistreat her so—never seemed to interest any of the columnists or cause any gossip. And yet Ritchie would often come on the set, insult her, throw a jealous tantrum and leave after he had reduced her to tears. A moment later, when it was time to film a scene, she was ready to work, all smiles. I was not surprised when I later heard her referred to as "The Iron Butterfly," although I was surprised to hear she found that amusing. I never thought she had much of a sense of humor. When we worked together she always objected to anyone telling a risqué story.

He said no more but feigned a moué of disdain and shrugged.

At the time Chevalier dissolved his MGM contract, Irving Thalberg, hearing from him that he planned to return to France, said, "You'll come back to Hollywood one of these days bigger than ever."

Back in Paris, Chevalier returned to his great love—the theatre. He toured the provinces, starred in a new Casino de Paris revue, made two French films, *L'Homme du Jour* and *Avec le Sourire,* and two films in London, *Break the News* and *The Beloved Vagabond.* When he arrived in England to begin filming, he was accompanied by Nita Raya, a nineteen-year-old dancer he had met when she was appearing in the chorus of a Parisian production of *Broadway.* Miss Raya was his constant companion for the next decade.

Although all his post-Hollywood films eventually played in the U.S. before the outbreak of the war, none of them, except *Pièges,* a taut suspenser directed by Robert Siodmak, made much of an impression. Nevertheless, Ernst Lubitsch contacted him about starring with Carole Lombard in a comedy, *To Be or Not to Be,* that would spoof Hitler and the Nazi Party.

Robert Florey recalls that Chevalier told him about it during his last visit to Paris, just before France fell. "While I was in Paris," Florey said, "Chevalier invited me to see his show from the wings of the Casino de Paris, and afterwards we went to a rue Blanche bistro with his friend and secretary Max Ruppa. Chevalier, always a worrier, spoke about Munich and what might happen soon. He spoke about his friendship and his admiration for Lubitsch and how much he had enjoyed working with him and his *gemütlich* way of doing things on the set. And he was hoping that any minute he would be called back to Hollywood."

INTERMISSION
(1940-1944)

In Paris, 1942

Celebrating his sixtieth birthday with musical comedy star Nita Raya, whose family he had sheltered from the Gestapo during World War II.

As he looked while entertaining, much against his will, during the Second World War

Paris has two monuments, the Eiffel Tower and Maurice Chevalier. Frenchmen love both dearly.

—JEAN COCTEAU

While waiting for word that Ernst Lubitsch was ready to begin production on his anti-Nazi comedy, Chevalier remained a headliner at the Casino de Paris, playing to the eve-of-war audience that seemed to live as if there would be no tomorrow. Before too long the tomorrow every Frenchman dreaded arrived and, as the German Panzer divisions invaded France, the big exodus from Paris began. Chevalier cabled Lubitsch he would be unable to accept his offer (Jack Benny got the part); his main concern was Nita Raya and her parents, who were Rumanian Jews.

He got them out of Paris and they took refuge at his farmhouse at La Bocca, near Cannes. It was located within the boundaries of that little strip of territory known as Free France. Chevalier's abrupt Paris departure, and his failure to return there to entertain his conquered countrymen, was attacked in the Nazi-controlled newspapers. One particularly impious story said, "Nearly every important entertainer who has any allegiance to his country is here (Paris) helping restore the faith of their compatriots, but the cowardly Chevalier remains on the Riviera with his Jews."

Fearing more such reports might endanger Miss Raya and her parents, he returned to Paris to play a three-week nightclub engagement. He also agreed to go to Germany where, at Alten Grabow, the prison camp where he had been interned during World War I, he performed one show. His condition: that ten prisoners of his selection, Parisians from Ménilmontant and Belleville, be released and allowed to return to their families. The Nazis met this stipulation and they promised still more prisoners would be released if he agreed to perform in Berlin. Part of the persuasion included a personal invitation from German actor Emil Jannings, who had been a top star at Paramount when Chevalier first arrived in Hollywood. He declined the German offers, however, and returned to La Bocca.

He was continuously hounded, not only by the Nazis and their propaganda, but also by members of the underground, particularly those of the Maquis resistance movement. The Nazis, and the underground, misquoted him—and one broadcast, heard in Switzerland and Great Britain, announced he had been slain by members of the Maquis movement for being a collaborator. This had occurred after he had again returned to Paris and fulfilled a six-week nightclub engagement after Miss Raya and her parents had been threatened by the Gestapo and promised even worse treatment if he refused to work. Later U.S. newspapers carried a report of a German broadcast which announced he had been condemned to death by the liberationists and that his execution, being beaten to death with blunt instruments and brass knuckles, had been carried out.

But when Paris was liberated, he turned up at his apartment where Paramount News shot footage of him (some of which only recently turned up in the documentary film *The Sorrow and the Pity*). The French publication *Ce Soir* carried a front page editorial about Chevalier that helped clear up some of the lies which had been circulated about him by the Nazis. And after an investigation of his wartime activities was made by General Eisenhower's staff, he joined Marlene Dietrich and Noel Coward at the Paris branch of the Stage Door Canteen and showed up, almost nightly, to help entertain the Allied troops.

He marched in the big Peace Parade in Paris, along with French soldiers and liberationists. Parisians, who had lined the boulevards to cheer the marchers, recognized and singled him out for special accolades that helped restore his self-confidence. Restored to his former prestige in the eyes and minds of his countrymen, he was ready to return to being an entertainer when the war ended and the world was ready to laugh again.

With Gracie Fields in London, 1940

THE GRAND YEARS
(1945-1972)

Entertaining at NYC's April in Paris Ball in 1961

If I had a son I would tell him that my thought is that in any kind of regime, a man who chooses to do a job in which he makes a living has to love that work, has to live the work that gives him food. I would tell him to be careful and choose what he would like best, and try to do his job better than the neighbor.

—MAURICE CHEVALIER.

Chevalier had a dream of doing a one-man show which he could present and tour with, motivated by public demand and his mood. It was a good two years after the end of the war before he got the show on the road.

He starred in René Clair's delightful comedy *Le Silence Est d'Or* as a movie director in the days of silent films. It was called *Man About Town* when it was released in the U.S. and it is the film that made Chevalier "box office" again. Soon after it was completed, he and Nita Raya came to a parting of ways and she married a man some thirty years younger than he was.

He arrived in New York aboard the *Queen Elizabeth* on March 1, 1947, and a little more than a week later opened his one-man show at the Henry Miller Theatre. For his first visit to the U.S. since the mid-1930's, he wore lapel ribbons for the *Croix de Guerre* and the *Legion d'Honneur* medals he had been awarded by the French government after World War I.

Brooks Atkinson, in *The New York Times*, noted that the first-night capacity audience was not unaware of all the ghosts hovering in the wings and backstage. He also wrote, "His smile is still as wide and glowing as the sunrise. The thick underlip still curls down. The eyes are laughing. His style is casual and jaunty, and he still sings infectiously on about five notes like one whose traveler's tales are set to music."

After his successful Broadway return, Chevalier returned to Hollywood to record an English-language narration for *Man About Town*, which RKO released.

His good friend Robert Florey recalls the occasion:

When he returned here he was a changed man. He had mellowed. Slightly aged, approaching sixty, the war years and the difficulties he had encountered then and afterwards had quieted him down. He was grateful to be so well received at a party we had given for him at Romanoff's.

A deal at MGM, to play Jane Powell's father in a musical, fell through so he again toured with his one-man show. He played Broadway again in 1948 and then returned to Europe. He made several films in France. In April, 1951, as he was preparing for another U.S. tour, he learned from newspaper headlines that he had been denied a visa because of his alleged Communist affiliations.

Because he had been one of the first "names" to endorse the Stockholm Peace Appeal, which demanded the banning of the atomic bomb by all nations, he was, in the minds of the government officials of the McCarthy era, subversive. His appeal to U.S. Attorney General J. Howard McGrath was denied after he had admitted publicly that he had indeed signed the Peace Appeal petition.

"Yes, I did sign it," he declared, "and in good faith, believe me. Millions of Frenchmen have signed it. Someone came around asking if I was against the atomic bomb no matter who used it and, well—nobody likes the atom bomb, so I signed it. But had I known what would happen I would still have signed . . ."

Chevalier was not alone. Many Americans, like Ethel Barrymore, had also signed and brought the wrath of their government down on their heads and all lived to appear less foolish than the government that censured them.

Denied entry to the U.S., Chevalier toured Canada and played to packed houses in Ottawa, Montreal and other cities. He never once criticized the U.S. for its decision and always maintained the whole thing was a mistake; a misunderstanding which would, in time, work itself out. His inability to return to Hollywood regrettably cancelled a film he was to make for Billy Wilder, *A New Kind of Love* (which was not the 1963 film with the same title in which he made a cameo appearance).

Chevalier continued his around the world tour with his one-man show, and then in 1952, while in France for a vacation, he gave his summer home at La Bocca to the French Society of Authors, Composers and Music Publishers for them to use permanently as a retirement home for needy members. In 1954, he again applied for a U.S. visa which was denied because it was "contrary to the best interests of the U.S." The denial was contrary to the best interests of Columbia Pictures because producer William Goetz wanted Chevalier in Hollywood to act as co-writer and technical consultant on a film to be based on his life story for which Danny Kaye had already been signed to play the lead.

But by the time his name was officially cleared

Showing off for reporters aboard *Queen Mary* in 1947

of any Communist attachment and he was granted a visa, in early 1955, Danny Kaye was involved with another film, Goetz was preoccupied with other projects and the Chevalier biography film was permanently shelved. But this disappointment turned out to be of small moment since no film story of his life could have possibly generated the excitement Chevalier, in person, was generating around the U.S.

After playing his one-man show on Broadway, at the Lyceum, for six solid sold-out weeks, and entertaining after the theatre with a show at the Waldorf-Astoria, he starred in a television spectacular, played four weeks in Las Vegas and returned to Hollywood to star in another television spectacular.

Of his 1955 return to Broadway, Richard Hayes, writing in *Commonwealth,* said:

> We have seen in our time so much grubbiness and concocted talent and meretricious beauty—so many bright morning faces on which neither time nor experience nor suffering will leave a mark—that what astonishes us in the face of a Chevalier (or a Garbo, a Dietrich, a Chaplin) is simply this: its wisdom. I do not mean knowledge; I mean *wisdom;* awareness of what we love and value, compassion and sensitivity, the unbought graces of life (if you will), harmonious *dans le vrai . . .*
>
> He is shrewd too, with that preternatural French sagacity—he knows that personality is one thing, and art another; that certain kinds of experience (pathos, for example) are not for him. He entertains but he does not trifle; he is intent on giving value for value; there is respect and civility in everything he does, and though he may occasionally be indecent, he is not even brushed by the wing of vulgarity.

And, in the New York *Times,* Lewis Funke asked:

> Has there ever been a more ingratiating, more infectious performer in show business than this Maurice Chevalier, this symbol and personification of all that is meant by the phrase "Gay Paree"? Has there, indeed, ever been anyone more indomitable?

On the 1955 telecast of the Academy Awards, Chevalier sang one of the nominated songs, "Something's Gotta Give," and presented the writers of the winning song, "Love Is a Many Splendored Thing," with their Oscars. Two years later, on another Oscarcast, he presented the Award for the Best Song, "All the Way," again.

In France, in 1957, a mature Chevalier offered movie lovers a delightful performance in Billy Wilder's sparkling comedy, *Love in the Afternoon.* That film was directly responsible for his triumphant return to Hollywood for *Gigi.* Not counting the special Oscar presented to him by Rosalind Russell after he had sung "Thank Heaven for Little Girls" during the 1959 Academy Award telecast, viewers saw *Gigi* being given nine Awards.

Days after that event, Chevalier said,

> What happened to me in the last eighteen months is still unbelievable—like a dream. That night of the Oscar awards was wonderful. To have that great actress, Rosalind Russell, come out and say the things about me she did before giving me the Oscar, I really felt so moved that I didn't know how to answer her. Afterwards, on the plane to Chicago, I didn't sleep—but not because I couldn't. I didn't want to sleep—I wanted to savor and treasure every moment of that night.

Of Chevalier's record appearance at the Greek Theatre in Los Angeles, when there wasn't an

With Sophie Tucker on a TV spectacular

Recording *I'd Rather Be Rich* with Robert Goulet and Andy Williams

With Edith Piaf

With Shirley Bassey, being greeted by Queen Mother Elizabeth

With Duke Ellington at the musician's seventieth birthday celebration in Paris—1969.

unsold seat for any performance, playwright-columnist Patterson Greene, in the *Los Angeles Examiner*, wrote:

> Forty-six hundred friendly customers gave Maurice Chevalier a prolonged and resounding welcome when he came upon the stage last night. This was the Chevalier of happily remembered past years—the Chevalier of "Louise" and "Valentine." But within an hour the plaudits had reached a second peak, and this was even more impressive because it was for the Chevalier today who has substituted warmth, gentleness and occasional wistfulness for the stinging wit and Gallic insouciance of times gone by. It is a change from high summer to mellow autumn.

Posing with a 1930 portrait

President Eisenhower welcomed him to the White House after that and, later, in Paris, he hosted a charity ball and sang "Ma Pomme" with President Charles de Gaulle. Then he came back to Hollywood to make *Can-Can* and celebrated his seventy-first birthday while it was in production. Said co-star Frank Sinatra, "This cat's really a gasser. He's got the market cornered on youth!"

A year later he worked with his good friend Charles Boyer for the first and only time in *Fanny*. During the filming at Cassis, Chevalier said:

> I'm not ashamed to play old men. To me, it is sad when an actor is afraid of growing old. My aim is to be as natural now as I was at twenty, but, I want to be honest about it. Take the song, "I'm Glad I'm Not Young Anymore"; I can't believe that anyone is ever really happy not to be young. Still, I can sing the words and smile, because, after all, we must accept things as they are.

None of his subsequent film appearances topped his triumphs in *Gigi* and *Fanny* but his continuous tours with his one-man shows kept him active and acclaimed internationally.

On his birthday in 1965, he was asked how it felt to be 77. "Not bad," he replied, "considering the alternative." And, with much candor, he added, "What keeps me at the top of my line is to be alone on the stage. I've got to be satisfied to be Maurice Chevalier. And I have been for a very long time. But now I must begin to think of the problem of my exit—it is the only future I have to discuss. It is so important for me to leave the table before I end up under it!"

During the 1967–1968 season, he set forth on his "farewell tour." He was eighty years old and fulfilled a marathon schedule that would have put a much young entertainer not under the table but

On the David Frost television show

31st Annual Awards—with his honorary special Oscar

Visited backstage by Jacqueline Kennedy in April 1965

Autographing copies of his book in San Francisco in 1970

With Fernandel after attending the funeral of Henry Varna, the manager of the famed Casino de Paris in April 1969

Chevalier's 1970 Christmas card

At home, in his study, 1970

most probably under the sod. It started in a rainstorm at the Expo '67 in Montreal, then covered twenty-two U.S. cities in two months. Between performances he spent a day in Los Angeles with Ingrid Bergman, an evening in Kansas with former President Harry S. Truman, and, a weekend at Hyannisport with the Kennedy clan. After playing in England, the Scandinavian countries, Amsterdam and Vienna, he turned up in New York where he made his last appearance on Broadway the night he accepted a special Tony Award from his beloved friend and former co-star Audrey Hepburn. After South America, and before the last lap, which would include sixty cities in Spain and Italy, he returned to Paris for his eightieth birthday celebration, held at the Lido. Flanked by Claudette Colbert and Noel Coward, he listened, misty-eyed, as Charles Trenet called him "the greatest master of the *chanson*—the Eiffel Tower of the *chanson*."

And indeed he was the one who pioneered the international one-man show and who paved the boulevards of the world with the applause and happy smiles of audiences who could anticipate the performers, including the famous French ones—Marcel Marceau, Edith Piaf, Charles Trenet, Jean Sablon, Lucienne Boyer and Suzy Solidor—who were all to come after him.

A 1916 postcard portrait of Mistinguett was Chevalier's 1960 Christmas card

Postcard of the famous statue in Brussels dressed as Chevalier which he sent to friends.

Audiences at the Theatre des Champs-Elysées applauded him for weeks and one night a stunned crowd heard him say, after singing his last song, "You've just seen the last recital I'll ever do on any stage anywhere."

He continuously received offers after that for "just one more tour" but, unlike Sarah Bernhardt, he rejected them all, most pleased to have been asked.

In December, 1971, aged eighty-three, he entered the Necker Hospital in Paris for treatment of a kidney ailment. He rallied after surgery to where he could sit up in a chair and eat. But he could only endure an artificial kidney for a few days and he suffered a heart attack. He died on January 1, 1972, and, a few days later, was buried beside his beloved La Louque.

The chief beneficiary of his fabulous estate was a pretty forty-year-old blonde widow, a one-time actress, Mrs. Odette Melier. She had been his closest friend and constant companion during his last years. To Madame Melier and her handicapped seven-year-old daughter Pascale whom Chevalier had loved and adored, he also bequeathed his home at Marnes-la-Coquette. Other beneficiaries were his two nephews, two former secretaries, several faithful servants and innumerable charities.

He exited from life with an enviable grace. "I have become a sort of International Frenchman," he once said. "And I feel a bit like the Eiffel Tower, always there when you look around."

He was, as usual, quite right. The Eiffel Tower is still there. And Maurice Chevalier is still here too: in the films he made which are constantly revived; in the songs he popularized and which no one else can sing quite as uniquely; in the charming books he wrote; and, in the hearts of all who have ever seen him and those who have yet to hear him on a record as he sings:

"Every little breeze . . .

Chevalier, meditating beside monument to his mother, "La Louque," at his home.

FILMOGRAPHY

PART ONE

SHORT SUBJECTS, FEATURETTES AND COMPILATION FILMS

El Cliente Seductor: with Rosita Dîaz Gimeno

SILENT:

TROP CRÉDULE 1908

A one-reel situation comedy, produced in France, directed by Jean Durand. With Joaquim Renez and Maurice Chevalier.

UN MARIÉE QUI SE FAIT ATTENDRE 1911

A one-reel slapstick comedy, produced in France, directed by Louis Gasnier. With Max Linder and Maurice Chevalier.

LA MARIÉE RECALCITRANTE 1911

A one-reel slapstick comedy, produced in France, directed by Louis Gasnier. With Max Linder and Maurice Chevalier.

PAR HABITUDE 1911

A one-reel slapstick comedy, produced in France, directed by Max Linder. With Max Linder and Maurice Chevalier.

LA VALSE RENVERSANTE 1914

A one-reel comedy sketch, produced in France by Pathé, in which Mistinguett and Maurice Chevalier had appeared with great success at the Folies Bergère.

UNE SOIRÉE MONDAINE 1917

A one-reel comedy sketch, directed by Henri Diamant-Berger, actually photographed at the Folies Bergère, with Mistinguett and Maurice Chevalier.

LE MAUVAIS GARÇON 1921

A comedy drama in five reels, adapted from a play by Jacques Deval, produced, directed and written by Henri Diamant-Berger. With Edouard de Max, Pierre de Guingand, Marguerite Moreno and Maurice Chevalier (as a naïve young man whose awkwardness effects a happy ending to an affair in which his sister has been seduced by a brilliant clubman). Filmed in France.

LE MATCH CRIQUI-LEDOUX 1922

A one-reel comedy, produced in France, directed by Henri Diamant-Berger. With Maurice Chevalier as an opinionated spectator involved in prizefight contretemps.

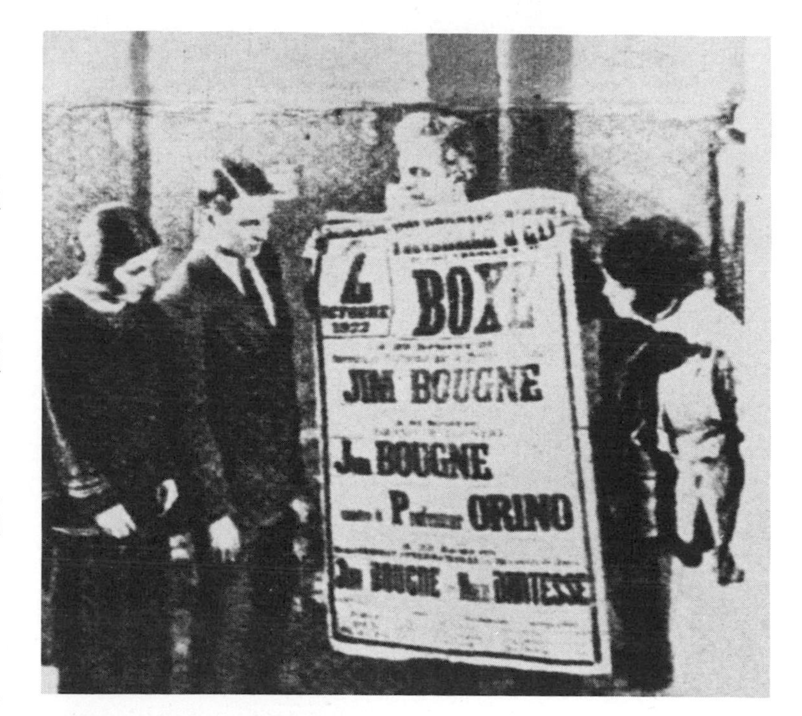

Jim Bougne Boxeur (1923)

Toboggan (Battling Georges): 1932

Par Habitude (1911)

This clip of Chevalier's silent film, *La Mariée Recalcitrante*, was used in *Paris 1900*.

Bonjour New York!: with his wife, director Robert Florey, and crew

GONZAGUE 1923

A situation comedy in three reels, produced, directed and written by Henri Diamant-Berger. With Marguerite Moreno, Albert Préjean and Maurice Chevalier (as a lovesick swain who poses as a piano tuner to be near the girl he loves at a dinner party to which he is invited to be the fourteenth guest by a superstitious host). Filmed in France.

L'AFFAIRE DE LA RUE DE LOURCINE 1923

A situation comedy in three reels, produced, directed and written by Henri Diamant-Berger. With Odette Florelle, Marcel Vallée and Maurice Chevalier (as an inveterate collegiate who, after a night of revelry at an annual college dinner, awakens with a hangover and reads a newspaper account of the grisly murder of a laundress, a crime he thinks he and his friend may have committed until he realizes it's an old newspaper he has been reading). Produced in France. Later rewritten and remade by Hal Roach as a Laurel and Hardy comedy.

PAR HABITUDE 1924

A three-reel comedy, produced, directed and written by Henri Diamant-Berger. With Georges Milton, Pauline Carton and Maurice Chevalier (as an absent-minded boulevardier who sublets his apartment, misses his train, goes on the town and then returns to his flat where, without ever remembering or meeting them, he manages to make his new tenants' lives miserable before departing the following day). Produced in France and a remake of his 1911 one-reeler in which he supported Max Linder. A U.S. version, produced by Hal Roach, starred Charley Chase.

JIM BOUGNE BOXEUR 1924

A three-reel comedy made in France and produced, directed and written by Henri Diamant-Berger. With George Milton, Odette Florelle, Martinelli and Maurice Chevalier (as a love-smitten young man who masquerades as a famous prizefighter to be near the girl he loves and is forced into the ring to fight with a real champion, Léon Journée—who *was* the heavyweight champion of France in 1924).

SOUND:

BONJOUR NEW YORK! 1928

A three-reel travelog, produced by Paramount for distribution in Europe, directed by Robert Florey. With Maurice Chevalier and his wife, Yvonne Vallée, playing themselves (and being photographed arriving by ship and then discovering the wonders of New York).

EL CLIENTE SEDUCTOR 1931

A two-reel Spanish language film, produced by Paramount at their Joinville Studios in France, directed by Florian Rey and Richard Blumenthal. With Imperio Argentina, Rosita Díaz Gimeno, Charles Martinez Baena, Carmen Navascués and Maurice Chevalier (as a resourceful boulevardier who manages to meet and romance three lovely ladies he encounters at a sunny sidewalk cafe during a summer afternoon).

THE STOLEN JOOLS (a/k/a THE SLIPPERY PEARLS) 1931

A two-reel comedy, privately produced by the Masquers Club of Hollywood and directed by William McGann, in which more than forty name players appear as themselves, policemen, newspaper reporters and other citizenry involved in the mystery of who stole a pearl necklace. In one sequence, Maurice Chevalier, playing himself, sang snatches of "It's A Great Life If You Don't Weaken" (one of his songs from *Playboy of Paris*). Shown first-run in theatres throughout the U.S. during the week of April 4, 1931, collections for the N.V.A. charity (National Vaudeville Association) were made in theatres immediately after its screening.

In *The New York Times*, Mordaunt Hall said,

> It is an amusing piece of work in which Norma Shearer's jewels are supposed to have been stolen and a police inspector in various disguises visits the different screen players who are supposed to have been at a dance where the jewels were missed. Wallace Beery opens the proceedings as a police sergeant and Bert Lytell comes on after the sketch and makes a plea for donations from the audience. (This subject was made to assist the National Vaudeville Association in swelling its benevolent fund.)

L'Affaire de la Lourcines (1923): Chevalier peering out of wardrobe

El Cliente Seductor: with Imperio Argentina and Carlos Martinez Baena.

El Cliente Seductor (1931): with Carmen Navascués and Rosita Díaz Gimeno

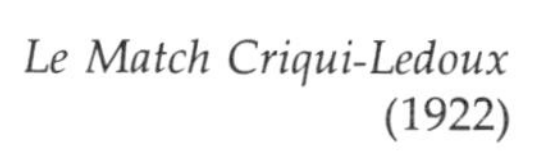

Le Match Criqui-Ledoux (1922)

Une Soirée Mondaine (1917): with Mistinguett

TOBOGGAN (BATTLING GEORGES) 1932

A one-reel charity promotion film, made in France, released by the Gaumont-France Film Aubert, and directed by Henri Decoin. With Arlette Marchal, Raymond Cordy, Paul Amiot, Sophie Duval, François Deschamps, John Anderson and Maurice Chevalier (shown sparring in a gymnasium and then as a cheering spectator at one of Georges Carpentier's boxing matches before making a plea to French audiences for contributions to a national charity for orphans.)

PARIS 1900 1950

A 76-minute documentary, written and directed by Nicole Vedres, with English adaptation by John Mason Brown and narrated by Monty Woolley. The footage covered a fourteen year period in French history (1900 to 1914) and showed glimpses of Maurice Chevalier, Mistinguett, Renoir, Rodin, Leon Blum, Jean Jaurès, Georges Carpentier, Claude Debussy, André Gide, André Mayol, Lucien Guitry, Cecile Sorel, Leo Tolstoy, Paul Valéry, Bleriot and Buffalo Bill. On the soundtrack the voices of Caruso and Sarah Bernhardt are heard.

RENDEZVOUS AVEC MAURICE CHEVALIER 1957

Six short subjects, originally made for television, compiled for theatrical showings in France. Directed by Maurice Regamey and released by Gaumont Production Distributors, it was ostensibly put together to cash in on Chevalier's fiftieth year in motion pictures. It did very little commercially and was quickly withdrawn. Two of the sequences included were pilots for a tv series which was never sold. Among the celebrities seen with Chevalier: Micheline Dax, the Marquis de Cuevas, Hubert de Givenchy, Eddie Constantine, Genevieve Page, Edith Piaf, Gilbert Becaud, Michele Morgan, Jacques Pills and Michele Arnaud.

NOTE:

For the erudition of film buffs who delight in "name dropping" film casts, here's a listing of many of the players who appear in *The Stolen Jools:* Robert Ames, Richard Barthelmess, Warner Baxter, Wallace Beery, Joe E. Brown, Charles Butterworth, Gary Cooper, Joan Crawford, Bebe Daniels, Claudia Dell, Richard Dix, Fifi D'Orsay, Irene Dunne, Douglas Fairbanks, Jr., Frank Fay, Louise Fazenda, Mitzi Green, Wynne Gibson, William Haines, Oliver Hardy, Hedda Hopper, Eddie Kane, Buster Keaton, Stan Laurel, Winnie Lightner,

Edmund Lowe, Ben Lyon, Bert Lytell, Victor McLaglen, Polly Moran, Jack Oakie, Eugene Pallette, Edward G. Robinson, Charles "Buddy" Rogers, Norma Shearer, Lowell Sherman, Barbara Stanwyck, George E. Stone, Lilyan Tashman, Bert Wheeler, Robert Woolsey, Fay Wray and Loretta Young.

COMMENTS:

Maurice Chevalier had little regard for films in 1908 when he worked as a comedy extra and was paid a few francs for his efforts. Later, however, he admitted that he had learned a great deal about comedy, especially timing and pantomime, from the legendary French genius Max Linder, with whom he had worked in several one-reelers. But he was far from a sensation in his early silent comedies and in 1917, after he was a well-established theatrical personality, he was still only paid a mere 75 francs for his work in *Une Soirée Mondaine*.

Four years later, however, he was paid 1,000 francs a day for appearing in *Le Mauvais Garçon* which led to his receiving film offers from the U.S. which he declined because he still felt that films

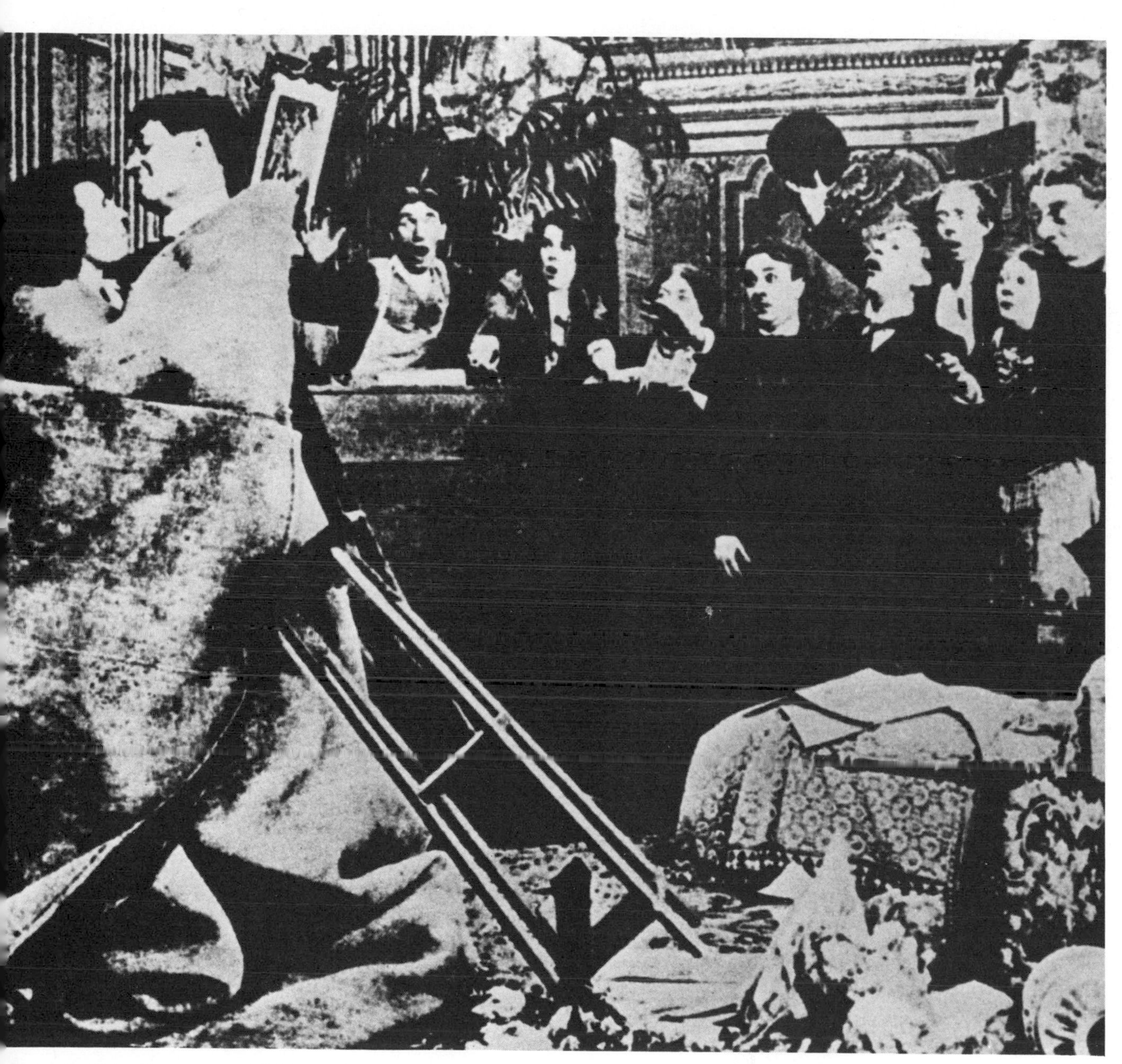

La Valse Renversante (1914): with Mistinguett

were not his forte. He had, nevertheless, signed a long-term contract with Henri Diamant-Berger to make three-reel comedies.

Said Henri Diamant-Berger, just a few weeks before his death in 1972:

> When Jesse Lasky came and signed Chevalier for Paramount, it was with my consent. I could not stop him with my little contract for three-reelers while he could become an international star and make real money in the States. Later, in 1934, while I was visiting my friend Lubitsch, who was directing Maurice in *The Merry Widow*, I gave him back his contract on the set in Hollywood.

At one time or another, several of Chevalier's silent comedies had U.S. showings in major cities and at least two of them were later remade by Hal Roach as vehicles for Stan Laurel and Oliver Hardy and Charley Chase.

Perhaps the most intriguing of Maurice Chevalier's short sound films is the Spanish language *El Cliente Seductor*. It never had a theatrical showing in the U.S. although it was very popular throughout Europe during the time of its release and even now turns up occasionally on a film retrospective program as a curiosity. Other than the fact that Chevalier appeared in it after becoming a major star and it's the only film he made exclusively in the Spanish language, is the intriguing casting of his three leading ladies, all very distinct personalities in their own right, who each deserves a word:

Imperio Argentina, who was married to Florian Rey (who co-directed *El Cliente Seductor*), later became Spain's foremost feminine star in features and short subjects which were almost exclusively directed by her husband, considered the country's leading director throughout the 1930's.

On location for *Bonjour New York!* with his wife, director Robert Florey (seated) and crew in October 1928

Rosita Díaz Gimeno, pretty and delightfully clever in a unique series of witty situation comedies, was Spain's most popular leading lady in the early 1930's and she later worked in Hollywood, most notably at Fox studios, where she appeared in many Spanish language versions of U.S. films.

Carmen Navascués, one of Spain's most celebrated beauties, dabbled in film work, decorated European fashion magazines as one of the best dressed women in international social circles and remained in the public eye because of her adventures as one of Europe's most successful and notorious courtesans. In the early 1940's she topped these triumphs by becoming the alluring and constant companion of the exiled King of Spain.

In recalling the making of *Bonjour New York!*, its very talented director, Robert Florey, told us,

In 1928, I had just finished directing some of the first talkies produced at the Paramount Astoria Studio in New York *(Night Club; The Hole in the Wall,* with Claudette Colbert and Edward G. Robinson; and F. Scott Fitzgerald's *The Pusher)* and was preparing *The Cocoanuts* for the Marx Brothers, when Walter Wanger, with whom I was riding in a taxi from New York to Long Island, said: "Do you know Maurice Chevalier?"

I told him that I had met Maurice in Paris in 1920, or early 1921, and had seen him on the French stage for several years previously. Chevalier, on his way to Hollywood with his wife, Yvonne Vallée, was going to spend a week in New York, and Wanger conceived the idea of taking advantage of his presence for making a short film which could be immediately exploited not only in France but also in other countries where French is spoken.

"Chevalier will arrive day after tomorrow; go and meet him at the French pier at 10 P.M. and talk to him about it. Of course this picture will not be included in his contract," said Wanger.

Bonjour New York!: with Al Wetzel, cameraman, and director Robert Florey aboard a Fifth Avenue bus.

With director Florian Rey on the set of *El Cliente Seductor* (1932).

Un Mariée Qui Se Fait Attendre (1911): with Georges Milton and Marguerite Moreno

"How long will it be and what will Chevalier do in it?" I wanted to know. Wanger answered, "It should run about from 20 to 30 minutes, and we have time to concoct something until he arrives."

At that time no talking films had been produced in France and very few of the theatres there were equipped for sound—mostly in such cities as Paris, Marseille, Bordeaux, and perhaps three or four in Belgium, Switzerland, etc., where American sound pictures were shown with superimposed French titles.

I told Chevalier that the studio was anxious to make a semidocumentary film of his impressions of New York, in which his voice would be heard for the first time on the screen—that was the only idea that I had been able to come up with!—and Chevalier was delighted, thinking perhaps that this might take but a few hours and give him a chance to see New York before going to California. [Actually, working from 7 A.M. until 4 P.M., it took four days.]

We shot some closeups and medium shots (two cameras) of Chevalier at the studio talking to "his" public about his trip, his impressions of New York, etc. to open and close the film. At the end of his introduction, he told the audience to come with him and visit the big city—he would be the guide—and the camera went all over from Wall Street to the Bowery, Chinatown, Broadway, the Statue of Liberty—lunch at the Lafayette—a trip on top of a bus down Fifth Avenue to Washington Square, Greenwich Village, on top of skyscrapers where, using a 25 mm. lens, we panned from a close shot of Maurice straight down to the street below, and other shots vice versa. Yvonne and Maurice had snails for lunch and that gave us an amusing scene.

While shooting on top of a high commercial building we forgot the time. It was a Saturday, and the elevators ceased functioning after 12 o'clock. For some reason or other, no one came to warn us; the elevator boys went home, and we had to come down on foot. Chevalier kept his smile, but we were tired when reaching the street after carrying all the equipment.

It was a good thing that many scenes were shot with silent cameras, Chevalier's voice being used on a sound track, recorded at the studio, and covering the action; otherwise, we couldn't have transported the heavy sound equipment and cameras down.

Maurice's facial expressions as he discovered America while making *Bonjour New York!*, the visual gags he added, his reactions to certain types of people we met—all these helped our little film a lot. It was a novelty and for a French audience an interesting newsreel-travelog-documentary which should not be classified as a Maurice Chevalier film or as a Hollywood production any more than the one-hour tv shows of Chevalier inviting the audience to visit "La Louque," his home at Marnes la Coquette, are authentic motion pictures.

FEATURE FILMS AND GUEST STAR APPEARANCES

PART TWO

INNOCENTS OF PARIS

A PARAMOUNT PICTURE *1929*

With Sylvia Beecher

Produced by Jesse L. Lasky. Executive Producer, Adolph Zukor. Directed by Richard Wallace. Screenplay by Ethel Doherty and Ernest Vajda. Adapted by Ernest Vajda from a story, "Flea Market," by Charles E. Andrews. Titles for the silent version by George Marion, Jr. Photographed by Charles Lang. Art Direction by Hans Dreier. Music and Lyrics by Richard A. Whiting and Lee Robin. Musical Arrangements and Orchestrations by the Paramount Music Department under the supervision of Nathaniel W. Finston. Sound Recording by Western Electric. Sound Engineer, Franklin Hansen. Edited by George Arthur. Dances by Fanchon and Marco under the supervision of LeRoy Prinz. Filmed in Hollywood. 78 minutes.

SONGS:

"Wait Till You See My Chérie," "Louise," "It's A Habit of Mine," "On Top of the World" (all by Whiting and Robin); "Valentine," "Les Ananas" (the French version of "Yes, We Have No Bananas") and "Dites-Moi, Ma Mère" (three songs from his Paris repertoire), sung by Maurice Chevalier.

CAST:

Maurice Marny, MAURICE CHEVALIER; *Louise Leval,* Sylvia BEECHER; *Emile Leval,* Russell Simpson; *Monsieur and Madame Marny,* Mr. and Mrs. George Fawcett; *Monsieur Renard,* John Miljan; *Madame Renard,* Margaret Livingston; *Jo-Jo,* David Durand; *Jules,* Jack Luden; *Musician,* Johnnie Morris.

With Sylvia Beecher and David Durand

STORY:

Junk dealer Maurice Marny saves a boy thrown into the Seine by his suicidal mother but is unable to save her. Returning the boy Jo-Jo to his grandfather, Maurice becomes interested in the child's aunt, Louise Leval. Her father, however, bitterly opposes the romance.

While singing in the Flea Market, Maurice interests the Renards, who audition and engage him for a show they are producing. Jealous of the chorus girls working with him, Louise begs Maurice to renounce the theatre, but he refuses. Just before the show opens, Louise's father learns of her secret romance and, enraged, starts for the theatre, pistol in hand.

Realizing Maurice's life is in danger, Louise telephones the theatre and tricks him into a rendezvous and then has him arrested. She later effects his release by admitting her hoax was only an attempt to save him from her irate father.

At the theatre, Maurice sings, not as the mysterious prince, as he has been billed, but just as himself. "I am not a prince, but a junkman," he tells the audience. He then sings for the first and last time in a theatre, happily renouncing it for Louise.

COMMENTS AND CRITIQUES:

Enchanted with the songs composed for *Innocents of Paris,* especially "Louise," Chevalier was still reluctant to do the film, rightfully thinking the script inferior. But when Paramount, in what they considered a magnanimous gesture, agreed to include three specialty songs he had popularized abroad, he had a change of heart.

With Sylvia Beecher

Consequently his debut in a sound feature proved an auspicious beginning to a successful film career. Overnight, he became the first major star of U.S. sound films. His legendary triumph seems even more unique when you consider he was working with an inadequate script in a language he had not fully mastered and in a medium stumbling through a gauche transitional period when the industry had abandoned making silent screen masterpieces in favor of creating "all talking, all singing, all dancing" disasters.

Contemporary critics were not remiss in alerting the public to the Chevalier genius.

In *The Film Spectator,* Welford Beaton said:

Maurice Chevalier is going to be a sensational success on the screen. Just why Paramount should introduce him in one of the stupidest stories of the year, I do not know. But the fact that the picture is highly entertaining in spite of the story leaves no question regarding the ability of the young Frenchman as an entertainer. He is an artist. He has a magnetic personality, a sense of humor and a pleasing singing voice. And there is something more to him; something back of these externals; a quality that hints of pathos and human understanding. I believe that as his familiarity with the medium grows, and when stories are written that at least are intelligent, we will find that in Chevalier we have the nearest approach to a Chaplin that yet has been produced.

In *The New York Times,* Mordaunt Hall said:

That engaging and worldly-wise French entertainer, Maurice Chevalier, won the hearts of an audience last night by his singing and talking in a picture called *Innocents of Paris,* which was presented at the Criterion Theatre. Without Chevalier this latest specimen of audible films would be a sad affair, but with him, one is willing to pardon incongruities and banalities. He is the whole show, and when he is off the screen the suspense consists of waiting until he reappears, either to sing or talk in his charming manner.

In *Sound Waves,* Josef Berne said:

Possessing a pantomimic ability topped only by Charles Chaplin, a personality topped by no one living, a keen sense of humor and a rare histrionic talent, Maurice Chevalier is in every sense of the word, a master of his art. We predict if he is given good vehicles, within a very short time, Chevalier will become the idol of America.

In *The Film Mercury,* Tamar Lane said:

Chevalier is not only a gifted artist and an excellent actor but he has a magnetism and an individuality which win their way immediately into the hearts of the audience. If this writer is not greatly mistaken, Chevalier is going to be one of the most popular players in the films before the year is out.

By his charming, unaffected, happy-go-lucky portrayal in the role of the lowly junk dealer, Chevalier quickly sweeps aside the show-us attitude with which an audience greets any newcomer to the screen and before five hundred feet of film have passed through the projection machine he has completely won patrons as ardent admirers.

In the *Beverly Hills Script,* Rob Wagner said:

This French lad, recently imported to America to make cinema whoopee for Paramount, is just about the most magnetic chap who has come to the screen.

When Elinor Glyn added animal magnetism to biology under the unscientific but snappy term of *It,* she cited as examples of those possessing that quality one girl, Clara Bow, and one horse, Rex. I should like to complete the triptych with a man —Chevalier.

And, in the *Los Angeles Examiner,* Jerry Hoffman said:

Chevalier (pronounced Sha-val-yay) makes a definite impression with his personality in a little speech of introduction to the picture a la talkie. This introduction, with a few song numbers he delivers during the course of the production, gives the audience an idea of what a splendid artist Chevalier (pronounced Sha-val-yay) really is.

New Yorkers paid $5.50 and more to see Chevalier (pronounced Sha-val-yay) on the New Amsterdam Roof. And he was worth it. For the reason of his presence alone, *Innocents of Paris* is worth seeing.

With chorus

A PARAMOUNT PICTURE 1929

With Jeanette MacDonald

Produced and Directed by Ernst Lubitsch. Screenplay by Ernest Vajda and Guy Boulton. Adapted from a play, "The Prince Consort," by Leon Xanrof and Jules Chancel. Photographed by Victor Milner. Art Direction by Hans Dreier. Costumes by Travis Banton. Music and Lyrics by Victor Schertzinger and Clifford Gray, Orchestrations by the Paramount Music Department, Conducted by Victor Schertzinger. Sound Recording by Western Electric, Sound Engineer, Franklin Hansen. Film Cutter, Merrill White. Filmed in Hollywood. 10 Reels.

SONGS:

"Paris, Stay the Same," "Anything to Please the Queen," "Nobody's Using It Now" (sung by Maurice Chevalier), "Dream Lover," "March of the Grenadiers" (sung by Jeanette MacDonald), "The Love Parade" (sung by Chevalier and MacDonald), "Champagne" (sung by Lupino Lane), "Let's Be Common" and "Gossip" (sung by Lupino Lane and Lillian Roth).

CAST:

Count Alfred, MAURICE CHEVALIER; *Queen Louise,* JEANETTE MacDONALD; *Jacques,* Lupino Lane; *Lulu,* Lillian Roth; *Master of Ceremonies,* Edgar Norton; *Prime Minister,* Lionel Belmore; *Foreign Minister,* Albert Roccardi; *Admiral,* Carlton Stockdale; *Minister of War,* Eugene Pallette; *The Afghan Ambassador,* Russell Powell; *Cabinet Ministers:* Anton Vaverka, Albert de Winton, William von Hardenburg; *Ladies in Waiting:* Margaret Fealy, Virginia Bruce, Josephine Hall, Rosalind Charles, Helene Friend; *Priest,* Winter Hall; *Cross-eyed Lackey,* Ben Turpin; *Extra in Theatre Box,* Jean Harlow.

STORY:

Much to the despair of her cabinet members, Queen Louise rules her kingdom of Sylvania with a lonely heart until Count Alfred, her foreign emissary, returns from Paris in disgrace. After reading a detailed report of the Count's escapades, the Queen sends for him and asks him to demonstrate his prowess as a great lover. His exhibition is so effective, the Queen marries him.

Count Alfred is soon balking at taking orders from his wife although he keeps up appearances because he knows the Queen is trying to negotiate a loan from a foreign power. But when she orders him to attend the opening of the royal opera, he refuses. In despair, the Queen goes alone. And her sudden joy, when he does show up, is short-lived because the Count tells her he intends leaving in the morning for Paris, where he will seek a divorce.

Late that night the Queen comes to his rooms for the first time and implores him to stay. But until she promises to allow him to become King as well as her husband, he remains adamant. But once she capitulates, they embrace—and live happily ever after.

COMMENTS AND CRITIQUES:

In his first sound film, Ernst Lubitsch combined the best elements of sly, romantic comedy, for which he had gained a well-deserved international reputation, with musical interludes in completely cinematic terms—while most of his contemporaries, unable to cope with the techniques of cumbersome and crude sound equipment, were content to photograph their films in static stage terms. The result: a completely captivating film, somewhat ahead of its time, which is still superior

With Jeanette MacDonald

With Jeanette MacDonald

With Jeanette MacDonald

With Jeanette MacDonald

to all other film musicals produced in the late 20's.

Instinctively, Lubitsch also knew how to introduce and showcase Jeanette MacDonald in a way that made audiences respond to her beauty and believe that underneath her frigid facade a warm and sexually alluring woman waited to be awakened. And Maurice Chevalier proved to be so much the perfect foil for her that his performance in *The Love Parade,* and his equally adroit one in *The Big Pond,* won him a nomination for an Academy Award (ultimately won by George Arliss for his performance as *Disraeli*).

On November 19, 1929, Miss MacDonald appeared onstage at the Criterion Theatre in New York and briefly addressed the audience attending the charity premiere. Unable to appear, because of an injury to his hand sustained while making *The Big Pond,* Chevalier spoke to the audience from the screen in a specially filmed apologia in which he explained the reason for his absence and most charmingly thanked everyone for attending.

The following morning Manhattan film critics were jubilant.

In the *New York Times,* Mordaunt Hall said:

Ernst Lubitsch, the brilliant German director, has served Maurice Chevalier, the French entertainer, well in his talking and singing picture, *The Love Parade,* which was offered last night to an attentive, appreciative and notable gathering in the Criterion. It is a production worthy of M. Chevalier's talent and something widely different from his first audible venture, *Innocents of Paris.* It is a charming imaginary kingdom satire, interspersed with song, the music having been provided by Victor Schertzinger . . . In the first place, it is a finely directed film, and while it is the initial vocal subject made by Mr. Lubitsch, it reveals unmistakably that this Teutonic genius is not dismayed by the linking of the microphone with the camera. It is a real moving picture in the literal sense of the words, and Mr. Lubitsch has seized every opportunity to lift it out of any suggestion of sentimentality by bright satirical shafts.

The *Herald Tribune* allowed that:

Advance reports from Hollywood in regard to the excellence of *The Love Parade* were entirely justified at the Criterion last night, where the new work had its local premiere. Enriched by the two entirely winning performances contributed by Maurice

Chevalier and Miss Jeanette MacDonald, an agreeable score, an engaging story, and a general air of gayety and charm, the picture proved to be a thoroughly captivating musical entertainment that immediately becomes one of the things to be seen in this town.

The brilliant Frenchman is little, if anything, short of perfect. Always one of the most likeable and completely satisfactory of performers, he demonstrates here a gift for sly and engaging comedy of the deftest sort that makes his portrayal as irresistible a piece of work as either stage or screen has offered this season.

New York *Evening World's* nameless critic said:

Having been given a story worthy of his superb talents, Maurice Chevalier came to the Criterion Theatre last night in *The Love Parade*, a charming, sophisticated romance of a mythical kingdom, and you are hereby cautioned that you will see it remain at that theatre for the greater part of the winter, and perhaps all of it.

The picture is that good. It has everything commendable . . . But what is more important, the French star made this picture under the direction of Ernst Lubitsch and therefore was not only permitted to show, but was assisted in showing what he really can do with subtlety and humor. The combination is irresistible. Lubitsch and Chevalier are precious, the one paving the way and the other doing the stuff . . . On the occasion of the premiere of *Innocents of Paris* we reported that, in our opinion, Maurice Chevalier would in time be one of the greatest artists upon the screen. We repeat that now, only we redouble.

The New York *Daily News* added their enthusiasm:

For Chevalier we simply can't find enough superlative adjectives. He is utterly delightful, entrancing, enrapturing. His wink, his smile, his—what they call personality, his superb understanding of Lubitsch's tricky megaphone; his refreshing performance of the leading role in *The Love Parade* should add—and how!—to his fan mail. Chevalier, in our opinion, is the most vivid actor on the screen today.

After the opening of *The Love Parade* on the West Coast, in January, 1930, Louella Parsons, in the *Los Angeles Examiner*, said:

The disarming and engaging smile with which Maurice Chevalier delivers his complicated English in *The Love Parade* had the audience at the Paramount Theatre completely enthralled. Mr. Chevalier need only speak a few words with his delicious accent to hold interest, but when you add to his charm the smart, sophisticated comedy of Ernst Lubitsch you have entertainment that rates high.

We speak so lightly of personality that it is probably the most misused word in the English language. Yet it is M. Chevalier's personality that is

With Jeanette MacDonald

chiefly responsible for his great success. You can well understand why Paris looked upon him as the greatest entertainer in the French capital. When he sings a song he puts so much of himself into it that you care not what he sings so long as you can see him smile and hear his laugh.

In the *Los Angeles Times,* Edwin Schallert wrote:

It is to Chevalier, in the stellar role, Jeanette MacDonald in the feminine lead, and Lubitsch as contriver of many funny bits of business, situations and subtle innuendoes that the major share of the credit goes for the attractions possessed by this production. Chevalier has much greater opportunity to display his talents, and the magnetism of his personality, than in the earlier feature, *Innocents of Paris.* He is really ideal in his response to the Lubitsch direction. He is able to shade expressions, both facial and vocal, remarkably, and is responsible for pointing up many a humorous line.

PARAMOUNT ON PARADE

A PARAMOUNT PICTURE 1930

With Evelyn Brent in the "Origin of the Apache" number

Produced by Albert S. Kaufman. Production Supervisor, Elsie Janis. Contributing Directors: Dorothy Arzner, Otto Brower, Edmund Goulding, Victor Heerman, Edwin H. Knopf, Rowland V. Lee, Ernst Lubitsch, Lothar Mendes, Victor Schertzinger, A. Edward Sutherland and Frank Tuttle. Photographed by Harry Fishbeck and Victor Milner. Color sequences by the Technicolor Corporation. Choreography by David Bennett. Production Designer, John Wenger. Sound Recording by Western Electric. Sound Engineer, Harry M. Lindgren. Edited by Merrill White. Filmed in Hollywood. 128 minutes.

SUMMARY OF SEQUENCES AND SONGS:

SHOWGIRLS ON PARADE. Staged by David Bennett with Virginia Bruce and a bevy of chorus girls singing "We're the Show Girls" afterwards joined by the chorus boys for "Paramount on Parade," both songs by Elsie Janis and Jack King.

OPENING TITLES. Dissolve into Mitzi Mayfair dancing among a montage of studio shots.

INTRODUCTION. "We're the Masters of Ceremony," by Ballard MacDonald and Dave Dreyer, sung by Jack Oakie, Skeets Gallagher and Leon Errol.

LOVE TIME. Charles (Buddy) Rogers, Lillian Roth and chorus sing "Any Time's the Time to Fall in Love" by Elsie Janis and Jack King.

MURDER WILL OUT. A comedy sketch with William Powell and Eugene Pallette (as Philo Vance and Sergeant Heath), Clive Brook (as Sherlock Holmes), Warner Oland (as Dr. Fu Manchu) and Jack Oakie (as the victim).

ORIGIN OF THE APACHE. Maurice Chevalier and Evelyn Brent in a comedy sketch, directed by Ernst Lubitsch.

SONG OF THE GONDOLIER. A two-color Technicolor sequence with Nino Martini singing "Come Back to Sorrento" *(Torno a Sorrento)* by Leo Robin and Ernesto DeCurtis.

IN A HOSPITAL. A comedy sketch with Leon Errol, Jean Arthur, Phillips Holmes and David Newell.

IN A GIRLS' GYM. Jack Oakie and Zelma O'Neal sing "I'm in Training for You," by L. Wolfe Gilbert and Abel Baer.

THE TOREADOR. Kay Francis and the Marion Morgan Dancers with Harry Green singing "I'm Isadore, the Toreador," music from Bizet's *Carmen,* lyrics by David Franklin.

With Evelyn Brent

"My Marine": Stanley Smith, Fredric March, Ruth Chatterton, Stuart Erwin, and Gunboat Smith

THE MONTMARTRE GIRL. In a Parisian café a group of Marines, including Stuart Erwin, Stanley Smith and Fredric March, watch Ruth Chatterton sing "My Marine" by Richard A. Whiting and Raymond B. Eagan.

PARK IN PARIS. Gendarme Maurice Chevalier, patroling a Parisian park where lovers are embracing on every bench, sings "All I Want is Just One Girl," by Richard A. Whiting and Leo Robin. Staged by Ernst Lubitsch.

MITZI HERSELF. Mitzi Green in a reprise of "All I Want is Just One Girl" imitating Charlie Mack, of the team of Moran and Mack (The Two Black Crows), and Maurice Chevalier.

THE SCHOOL ROOM. Helen Kane teaching her class, which includes Jackie Searle and Mitzi Green, that "Boop, Boopa, Doop" is the answer to "What Did Cleopatra Say?" by Elsie Janis and Jack King.

THE GALLOWS SONG. In this two-color Technicolor sequence Dennis King, at the insistence of Skeets Gallagher, sings the Russian love song "Nichavo," by Mana-Zucca, while enroute to be hanged.

DANCE MAD. Nancy Carroll, Abe Lyman and His Orchestra, and chorus sing and dance "Dancing to Save Your Sole," by L. Wolfe Gilbert and Abel Baer.

DREAM GIRL. Skeets Gallagher, Gary Cooper, Richard Arlen, James Hall, Mary Brian, Fay Wray and Eugene Pallette introduce a two-color Technicolor sequence, costumed in the Civil War period, of Richard Arlen, Jean Arthur, Mary Brian, Virginia Bruce, Gary Cooper, James Hall, Phillips Holmes, David Newell, Joan Peers and Fay Wray harmonizing "Let Us Drink to the Girl of My Dreams," by L. Wolfe Gilbert and Abel Baer.

THE REDHEAD. Clara Bow, supported by Jack Oakie, Skeets Gallagher and a chorus of forty-two sailors, sings "I'm True to the Navy Now," by Elsie Janis and Jack King.

IMPULSES. George Bancroft, Kay Francis, William Austin, Henry Fink, Cecil Cunningham, Robert Grieg, Jack Pennick and Jack Luden in a comedy sketch about social manners.

THE RAINBOW REVELS. The finale, in two-color Technicolor, directed by Ernest Lubitsch, with Maurice Chevalier, and a chorus of girl chimney cleaners, singing "Sweeping the Clouds Away," by Sam Coslow.

PARAMOUNT EN PARADE

A French-language version of *Paramount on Parade* which utilized most of the American song sequences (dubbed) but redid the comedy sketches, was filmed at Paramount's studio at Joinville-le-Pont, in France. Jacques Bataille-Henri revised and translated the sequences involving French cast members Marguerite Moreno, Charles de Rochefort, Pierre Moreno, Saint-Granier, Louis Boucot, Alice Tissot, Madeleine Guitty and Elmire Vautier. Maurice Chevalier re-filmed his three sequences there (directed by Charles de Rochefort) and also Spanish, Italian, German and Roumanian versions. For the Spanish-language version, a mixture of sequences of the U.S. and France footage (mostly), some new scenes were shot in Hollywood with Jeanette MacDonald doing yeoman service as mistress of ceremonies (replacing Jack Oakie, Skeets Gallagher and Leon Errol) and singing in place of Nino Martini.

COMMENTS AND CRITIQUES:

Paramount on Parade was neither the best, the worst, nor the gaudiest of the all-star musical revues which began stupefying audiences with *The William Fox Movietone Follies of 1929,* released about sixteen months after *The Jazz Singer* opened. The cycle lasted a year and included Fox's less ponderously titled sequel, *Movietone Follies of 1930,* and their *Happy Days;* two Warner Bros.' vulgarities, *Show of Shows* and *On With the Show;* and, MGM's gloriously ghastly and glittering contribution, *Hollywood Revue of 1929*. Most of them experimented with two-color Technicolor sequences, juggled vaudeville sketches and, occasionally, dramatic readings, with song and dance numbers performed by virtually every contract player on the lot who was too flabbergasted to protest. They were all marvelously dreadful extravaganzas and very popular—in spite of critical forewarnings.

The all-star musical cycle had a resurgence during World War II with *Star Spangled Rhythm, Thousands Cheer, Thank Your Lucky Stars, Stage Door Canteen, Hollywood Canteen* and *Follow the Boys* which all had the effrontery to add a plot, of sorts, to the proceedings that automatically decreased the number of chances audiences had to revel in masochistic pleasure while watching one of their favorite stars

Skeets Gallagher, Clara Bow and Jack Oakie in "I'm True to the Navy, Now"

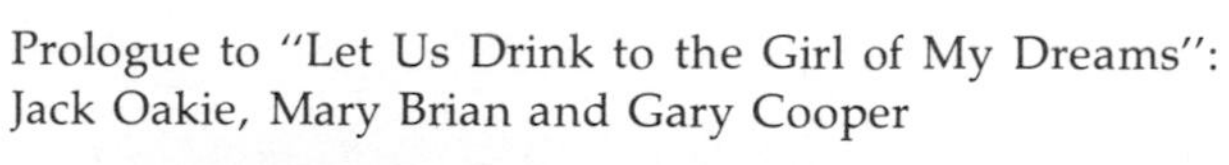

Prologue to "Let Us Drink to the Girl of My Dreams": Jack Oakie, Mary Brian and Gary Cooper

struggle through an unsuitable song and dance routine. This second cycle was so popular it lasted after the war and right into the McCarthy era with such eye-assaulting, ear-shattering entries as *Ziegfeld Follies, Till the Clouds Roll By* and *Starlift. Starlift,* just about the last all-star musical produced in Hollywood, couldn't have been more inappropriately titled because, cavalier as it sounds, it was released ('51) just about the time that the star system started to expire.

But in 1930, when *Paramount on Parade* was released, the star system was at its apex and the brightest member of its galaxy was Maurice Chevalier, who used his three opportunities in this film to charm audiences and the critics. In *The New York Times,* Mordaunt Hall said:

This jovial satire is beautifully staged, and virtually all the sketches are endowed with wit, surprises, competent acting and tuneful melodies. If there are scenes of dancing girls, Miss Janis has seen to it that they are never too lengthy to be tedious and she has wisely included three numbers with Maurice Chevalier, who, if anything, is perhaps even more engaging in these glimpses than in his own features; it is the type of work that is well suited to him.

M. Chevalier first gives an amusing travesty on the origin of the Apache dance. He is subsequently perceived as an *agent de police* in a Paris park, who satisfies himself as to the addresses and telephone numbers of some of the girls occupying the benches with their sweethearts. M. Chevalier's third sketch is a musical affair with chorus girls. It is all about "sitting on top of a rainbow and sweeping the clouds away." This particular sequence, like several others, is in Technicolor, with a rainbow of pretty girls. The colors may not be true to the prism, but here, at least, they are effective, although most of the tinted episodes in other parts of this picture are not in focus—or, they were not yesterday afternoon.

In *The Film Spectator,* Frank T. Daugherty said:

Paramount on Parade might be called a fair-to-medium Orpheum bill, and then again it might be called a rattling good trailer—and either one would be right. There are no particularly dull moments in it, and there are no particularly bright ones. I confess to a predilection for Little Mitzi (Green) in her imitation of one of the Two Black Crows; for George Bancroft's little play of society manners; and for Maurice Chevalier. I don't know why Chevalier, for I don't remember that he did anything; but even if he didn't, he does nothing better than anyone else, so I suppose that's the reason.

In the "Rainbow Revels" finale

THE BIG POND

A PARAMOUNT PICTURE 1930

With Claudette Colbert

Claudette Colbert, Marion Ballou and George Barbier

With Nat Pendleton in the French-language version

With Claudette Colbert in the French-language version

Produced by Monta Bell. Directed by Hobart Henley. Assistant Director, Bertram Harrison. Screenplay by Robert Presnell and Garrett Fort. Dialog by Preston Sturges and Robert Presnell. Based on the play, "The Big Pond," by George Middleton and A. E. Thomas. Photographed by George Folsey. Claudette Colbert's Costumes by Carolyn Putnam. Sound Engineer, Ernest Zatursky. Edited by Emma Hill. Filmed in New York at Paramount's Astoria studios. 85 minutes.

SONGS:

"Livin' in the Sunlight, Lovin' in the Moonlight" (by Al Lewis and Al Sherman), "This Is My Lucky Day" (by Lew Brown, B. G. DeSylva and Ray Henderson), "Mia Cara" and "You Brought A New Kind of Love to Me" (by Irving Kahal, Pierre Norman and Sammy Fain), sung by Maurice Chevalier.

CAST:

Pierre Mirande, MAURICE CHEVALIER; *Barbara Billings,* CLAUDETTE COLBERT; *Mr. Billings,* George Barbier; *Mrs. Billings,* Marion Ballou; *Toinette,* Andree Corday; *Ronnie,* Frank Lyons; *Pat O'Day,* Nat Pendleton; *Jennie,* Elaine Koch.

STORY:

While working as a guide in Venice, Pierre Mirande, scion of an honorable but war-impoverished French family, meets and falls in love with Barbara Billings, an American tourist. Her mother is captivated by Pierre but her father and Ronnie, her suitor, warn the stubborn Barbara that he is nothing more than a fortune hunter. Believing he can convince her of this, Mr. Billings offers him a job in his chewing gum factory which Pierre joyously accepts.

After he arrives in America and is quartered in a shabby rooming house, Pierre becomes disillusioned with his back-breaking factory job. Barbara assures him, however, that his opportunity for advancement will eventually present itself and he must be ready when it does. But Pierre is so physically exhausted at night that he's socially *de trop* at Barbara's parties. This seems to substantiate her father's accusations that he really doesn't care for her.

The following evening, as Pierre finishes work at the factory, Pat O'Day, the shop foreman, offers him a drink. But as he passes the bottle, it slips and breaks, accidentally soaking a case of gum samples with rum. Blamed for the mishap, Pierre is fired. But he later chances to chew a stick of the rum-soaked gum. Making a startling discovery, he hurries to the front office and sells Mr. Billings on his idea of manufacturing rum-flavored gum. The idea is accepted and he's hired to write the advertisements for the new product. Using the tune of a love song with which he had serenaded Barbara in Venice, he writes new lyrics which praise the pleasures of chewing rum gum.

Considering this exploitation of "their" song a personal insult, Barbara tells Pierre she is through with him and is going to marry Ronnie. But Pierre, now confident and aggressive, kidnaps her and sets forth on a combined honeymoon and business trip.

LA GRANDE MER

Simultaneous with making the English-language version of *The Big Pond,* a French-language version was also made at Paramount's Astoria studios on Long Island. Directed by Hobart Henley, with the assistance by Jacques Bataille-Henri who also trans-

With Claudette Colbert

lated the script. Barney Rogan edited this version but other technical credits are substantially the same. Maurice Chevalier, Claudette Colbert, Andree Corday and Nat Pendleton repeated their roles but other cast members included Henry Mortimer, Maude Allen, William Williams and Loraine Jaillet.

COMMENTS AND CRITIQUES:

By 1930 no one in the film industry doubted that sound films were here to stay. In an effort to keep their product on the international market, Hollywood studios experimented with dubbing their most important films in foreign languages. But the technique was far from perfected and the inconsistent synchronization of dialog and lip movements often had ludicrous results. A more satisfactory solution was needed and the most feasible one turned out to be making foreign-language versions of films concurrent with the English language ones. This necessitated importing writers, directors and performers who could perform the functions that their American counterparts could not. Occasionally, as in the instances of Charles Boyer, Danielle Darrieux, Joe May and a few others, it also brought the *emigré* into prominence with U.S. audiences. The big fallacy of this system was the fact that very few contract stars were bilingual and their replacement in foreign language films meant studios could not capitalize on their drawing power overseas. But name stars who were bilingual soon realized this asset was a distinct advantage when the moment to negotiate salary and contract options came around.

Maurice Chevalier, of course, was one such star. Already an established box-office personality in Europe, the French language versions of his Paramount films received the same lavish attention as the ones made for the U.S. market. So much so that Chevalier always maintained that the French language versions of his U.S. films were the superior versions. "These films," he recalled in 1960, "all had extra charm because we were able to use some little risqué bit of business or dialog which, because of censorship, we could not do in the films made for the American audience."

Critics found much to report on both versions of *The Big Pond.* In *The New York Times,* Mordaunt Hall said:

Above the tumult, the shouting, the slang, the wisecracking and crudities of the audible pictorial version of the play *The Big Pond* looms the figure of Maurice Chevalier, whose whole-hearted acting compensates in no small degree for the farcical extravagances in this unimaginative narrative.

Although most of its scenes are blunt, verging in some instances on slapstick, this *Big Pond* is the sort of comedy that is never tedious or annoying. In fact, it succeeded in making hundreds laugh at a late performance on Saturday. Nevertheless, considering what Ernst Lubitsch did with *The Love Parade,* it is disappointing to observe M. Chevalier with a millstone of a story. The small mercy for which to be thankful is that no sequence in this offering sinks to the depths of his first screen adventure, *Innocents of Paris.*

In the *Los Angeles Times,* Edwin Schallert said:

The Big Pond is really adroitly developed, despite a slight story, and it offers amusing touches, not just here and there but all along the line.

Chevalier, in one of the most sympathetic roles that he has yet played, is responsible for most of the fun, and is ever so likeable in this particular portrayal. For no special reason of plot he sings several songs. The numbers, "You Brought A New Kind of Love to Me" and "Livin' in the Sunlight, Lovin' in the Moonlight" are just his type.

In the August 20, 1930, issue of *Weekly Variety,* this review of the French language version appeared:

If they go for this in France the way an audience of cosmopolitan French (the genuine, students, affectationists, etc.) went for it at the première in the 55th Street Cinema, *La Grande Mer* will be more popular than the original *The Big Pond.* Chevalier puts so much vim into his mannerisms, with the native tongue elucidating, that a Yank foreigner can get an idea of what it is all about and enjoy the show.

That's the way it is all the way through, except judging from some of the high-pitched cackles of those fans who whispered in French, a lot of the dialogue for this overseas parcel must have the kick which had to be censored in the American lingo.

The vivacity of Maurice is everything in this. As has been noted, it reflects in the cast, inbuing the players with a liveliness which could not have reached the same maximum with another lead.

Miss Colbert is pretty and plays her French with a native fire. She does not sing, except a few bars

A PARAMOUNT PICTURE 1930

With Tania Fedor in the French-language version

With Stuart Erwin and O. P. Heggie

With Yvonne Vallee in the French-language version

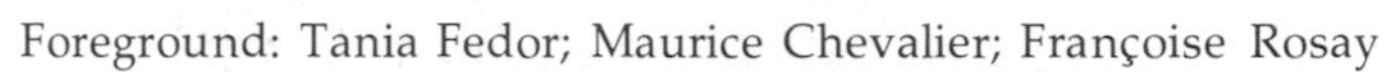

Foreground: Tania Fedor; Maurice Chevalier; Françoise Rosay

of the theme song in response to Chevalier. (Waly)

Produced and Directed by Ludwig Berger. Screenplay by Vincent Lawrence. Adaptation by Percy Heath. Based on the play, "Le Petit Café," by Tristan Bernard. Photographed by Henry Gerrard. Art Direction Supervisor, Hans Dreier. Music and Lyrics by Richard A. Whiting, Newell Chase and Leo Robin. Orchestrations and Arrangements by the Paramount Music Department under the supervision of Nathaniel W. Finston. Sound Recording by Western Electric. Sound Engineer, J. A. Goodrich. Edited by Merrill White. Filmed in Hollywood. 79 minutes.

SONGS:

"My Ideal," "It's a Great Life If You Don't Weaken" and "In the Heart of Old Paree" sung by Maurice Chevalier.

CAST:

Albert, MAURICE CHEVALIER; *Yvonne,* FRANCES DEE; *Philibert,* O. P. HEGGIE; *Paul,* Stuart Erwin; *Pierre,* Eugene Pallette; *Mlle. Berengere,* Dorothy Christy; *Mlle. Hedwige,* Cecil Cunningham; *Cadeaux,* Tyler Brooke; *Monsieur Bannack,* William Davidson; *Gastonet,* Charles Giblyn.

STORY:

Café owner Philibert plans for his daughter, Yvonne, to marry a wealthy Parisian although she is in love with Albert, one of his waiters. Soon after discharging him for being incompetent, Philibert learns that Albert is unaware of the fact that he is about to inherit a fortune. Conspiring to get part of his legacy, Philibert rehires Albert, at a substantial raise in salary, and signs him to a twenty-year contract which he's certain Albert will soon want to buy back.

Out of spite, Albert remains a waiter by day but revels in Parisian nightlife, accompanied by the gold-digging Mlle. Berengere. Furious because Albert has been ignoring her, Yvonne follows him one night on his nocturnal rounds of merry-making and becomes embroiled in a cat fight with Mlle. Berengere. Albert extricates her but in so doing is challenged to a duel by Monsieur Bannack.

On the morning they meet on the field of honor, Yvonne, fearing for Albert's life, tells Bannack he is merely a waiter, so the duel is called off. Indignant, Albert slaps his challenger, demanding satis-

With Frances Dee

With Eugene Pallette

faction. Yvonne saves him a second time by fainting. Rushing to comfort her, Albert realizes he loves her and can overlook the matter of defending his honor.

LE PETIT CAFÉ

Paramount's filmed-in-Hollywood French language version of *Playboy of Paris,* with dialog and lyrics by Jacques Bataille-Henri, was also directed by Ludwig Berger. Maurice Chevalier repeated his role of *Albert* and others in the cast included Yvonne Vallée, Emile Chautard, George Davis, André Berley, Tania Fedor, Françoise Rosay, Jacques Jou-jerville and André Bauge. Because Chevalier reprised his songs, with additional verses, this version ran 85 minutes.

With Stuart Erwin

COMMENTS AND CRITIQUES:

By not counting Chevalier's guest star appearance in *Paramount on Parade* or the foreign language versions of his films, *Playboy of Paris* was his fourth feature for Paramount. It was also the one film he had been keen to make.

While negotiating his contract with Jesse Lasky, the question of suitable scripts came up and Chevalier suggested that for his first U.S. film he do a remake of Max Linder's post-World War I comedy *Le Petit Café*. Although that film had been a tremendous success in France, it had done very little commercially when Pathé imported it in 1920. Lasky was skeptical but Chevalier remained adamant. So to placate their top money-making star, Paramount ultimately acquired the screen rights to it.

Filmed simultaneously in English and French-language versions, Chevalier and his partisans have always rightly assessed the French version superior. His wife, Yvonne Vallée, played the ingenue in this version and did so well that Paramount offered her subsequent assignments in their French-language films which she steadfastly declined.

In addition to singing three songs, Chevalier imbued *Playboy of Paris* with his insouciant personality and although, critically, it was not *l'immense succès* for which he had hoped, it does have its moments. Chief among them: a comedy sequence which ranks among the screen's funniest and proves that Chevalier, like Chaplin and other great comedians, was blessed with the true touch of comic genius. The sequence occurs in a wine cellar where he samples the contents of each barrel and apparises them as if he was judging a beauty contest and each cask was a contestant. The climactic moment, when he tastes, caresses and kisses a barrel of heady Burgundy, from which he gets a gurgle of appreciation, is hilariously brilliant. Unfortunately there were no other moments to equal this and the duelling sequence, at the end of the film, which *should* have topped this scene, was pedestrian and tasteless.

And reviews were, at best, lukewarm. In the New York *Times,* Mordaunt Hall said:

M. Chevalier gives another of his unfailing portrayals, with the result that it is an enjoyable picture, but nonetheless one that might have been greatly improved by more subtlety in the cinema script and by a more judicious selection of some of the supporting players.

In spite of its shortcomings, however, it is an infinitely better story than either *Innocents of Paris* or *The Big Pond*, but it lacks that sparkling quality with which Ernst Lubitsch endowed *The Love Parade.* Hence one hopes to see M. Chevalier in more pictures directed by the talented German.

In the *Los Angeles Examiner,* Louella Parsons reported:

> I doubt, without Chevalier, if the story could be classed as anything more than mediocre. With his occasional song and his always delightful accent, and his unerring comedy, *Playboy of Paris* is good fun. And Chevalier is always a personality we like to see.

After the New York opening of the French version, *Le Petit Café*, the January 28, 1931 issue of *Weekly Variety*, reported:

> First reaction after seeing this film is that Paramount is making a big mistake showing it in New York. It is so much better than the original English version and Chevalier's work in it is so much superior to that in any of his American films in English that his rep—for American films—may suffer.

And after *Le Petit Café* premiered in Paris, *Weekly Variety* noted that in France it was:

> A smash, breaking all local Paramount records, number of admittances for the opening day jumping from the preceding figure of 9,800 for *Love Parade* to the new figure of 11,200. Nothing better than this film could be devised to counteract any bad effects of the poor publicity Chevalier was given in his last trip. He throws off the ritz and gives up the classes for the masses.

With Frank Elliott, Erin La Bissoniere and Charles Giblyn

A PARAMOUNT PICTURE 1931

Produced and Directed by Ernst Lubitsch. Screenplay by Ernest Vajda and Samson Raphaelson. Adapted from the operetta, "The Waltz Dream," by Leopold Jacobson and Felix Doermann (Biedermann) and the novel, "Nex der Prinzgemahl," by Hans Müller. Photographed by George Folsey. Music and Lyrics by Oscar Straus and Clifford Grey. Musical Direction by Adolph Deutsch. Musical Arrangements by John W. (Johnny) Green and Conrad Salinger. Sound Engineer, C. V. Tuthill. Film cutter, Merrill White. Filmed in New York at Paramount's Astoria Studio. 88 minutes.

SONGS:

"That's the Army" and "Breakfast Table Love," sung by Maurice Chevalier. "Jazz Up Your Lingerie" sung by Claudette Colbert and Miriam Hopkins. "Live for Today" sung by Chevalier and Colbert.

CAST:

Niki, MAURICE CHEVALIER; *Franzi,* CLAUDETTE COLBERT; *Princess Anna,* MIRIAM HOPKINS; *Max,* Charles RUGGLES; *The King,* George Barbier; *An Orderly,* Hugh O'Connell; *Adjutant von Rockoff,* Robert Strange; *The Emperor,* Con MacSunday; *Lily,* Janet Reade; *Baroness von Halden,* Elizabeth Patterson; *Count von Halden,* Harry Bradley; *Joseph,* Werner Saxtorph; *Master of Ceremonies,* Karl Stall; *Bill Collector,* Granville Bates.

STORY:

Franzi, a pretty violinist, and Niki, an officer of the guards, maintain a blissful Vienna love nest until Niki is called to attend the needs of the visiting King and his daughter, Princess Anna. Misinterpreting Niki's mischievous smile, intended for Franzi, Princess Anna thinks he is patronizing her for being dowdy and unattractive. Overzealous in denying the accusation, Niki lavishly flatters the Princess and she promptly falls in love with him. A marriage is quickly arranged by the ecstatic King, who had feared his daughter was destined for spinsterhood. Afterwards, Niki blithely resumes his affair with Franzi.

Learning of their liasion, Princess Anna summons Franzi to the palace where they berate each other until Franzi takes pity on Anna and helps convert her from an ugly duckling into a lovely swan.

Miriam Hopkins and Claudette Colbert

With Claudette Colbert

With Claudette Colbert

CLAUDETTE COLBERT
CHARLIE RUGGLES MIRIAM HOPKINS
Music by OSCAR STRAUS

Irresistible! Gay Maurice, debonair as ever, laughing his way in and out of love as beautiful Claudette Colbert and Miriam Hopkins play at hearts with him. Produced by Ernst Lubitsch, whose sure deft touch and surprise situations make his pictures such a delight. You'll go out of the theatre feeling happy as a lark, a sparkle in your eyes, a song in your heart. It's *that* kind of picture—don't miss it! "*If it's a Paramount Picture it's the best show in town!*"

PARAMOUNT PUBLIX CORP. ADOLPH ZUKOR, PRES., PARAMOUNT BLDG., N. Y.

Leaving Niki a farewell note, which she has pinned to a garter, Franzi departs from Vienna. Infuriated, Niki confronts his wife but is so dazzled by her transformation that he forgets Franzi and decides life with a wealthy and beautiful Princess has its own advantages.

LE LIEUTENANT SOURIANT

Paramount's simultaneously filmed French-language version of *The Smiling Lieutenant*, also produced and directed by Ernst Lubitsch, for which Maurice Chevalier, Claudette Colbert and Miriam Hopkins repeated their roles and Jacques Bataille-Henri wrote the dialog and French song lyrics. 88 minutes.

COMMENTS AND CRITIQUES:

The reuniting of Ernst Lubitsch and Maurice Chevalier, as director and star, came at a most fortunate time. Until its release, critics were beginning to despair of the second-rate vehicles to which Hollywood's most popular male star had been relegated. *The Smiling Lieutenant* restored Chevalier's wavering *amour-propre* by charming critics and audiences. Only a few people realized it was a remake of *Ein Walzertraum*, a 1925 film, directed by Ludwig Berger and starring Mady Christians and Willy Fritsch, which, when released in the U.S. as *A Waltz Dream*, had been one of the most popular and acclaimed films imported from Germany during the 1920's.

The death of Chevalier's beloved mother, which occurred while *The Smiling Lieutenant* was in production, and his estrangement from his wife Yvonne Vallée who returned to France shortly after its completion and ultimately divorced him, were personal tragedies which in no way affected his screen work.

For years *The Smiling Lieutenant* was considered a "lost" film as no print of it was known to exist. Within the past few years, however, a print of the English-language version was discovered. Since then it has been shown at university film retrospectives and at revivals with great success. Because of its unavailability, many film historians had dismissed it as one of the lesser Lubitsch-Chevalier efforts. But a perusal of contemporary reviews, and box-office receipts, attests to how well it had been received and acclaimed.

In *The New York Times*, Mordaunt Hall, who had long hoped for a Chevalier-Lubitsch reunion, rhapsodized:

Wit and melody swing through Maurice Chevalier's latest picture, *The Smiling Lieutenant*, which is now adorning the Criterion screen. That cinematic artist, Ernst Lubitsch, supplies the rapier-like comedy and none other than Oscar Straus is responsible for the charming musical compositions . . . The wit

With Claudette Colbert

and melody coast mostly through M. Chevalier, whose smiling and singing are bound to appeal to all those who see this offering. He is a delight in all his scenes and, although a few stretches in which he does not appear are by comparison a trifle lethargic, Herr Lubitsch, in the greater part of this production, reveals himself to be once again a master of the microphone as well as of the camera.

In the *New York Herald Tribune,* Marguerite Tazelaar said:

Once more the combination of Maurice Chevalier and Ernst Lubitsch results in a piece of artistry, this one *The Smiling Lieutenant,* flawless in its manipulation and not far from perfect in performance . . . Oscar Straus' music needs no commendation. Once more you hear his haunting and lovely waltzes as well as a beautiful accompanying score. Among the new numbers are tuneful jingles you will soon hear over the radio no doubt . . . Chevalier was in perfect form, getting his effects over with the charm and humor that only he knows how to do.

In Los Angeles, *The Smiling Lieutenant* was roadshown at the Carthay Circle Theatre where it played twice daily after a lavish Hollywood première which commemorated Paramount's Twentieth Birthday Jubilee celebration. In the *Los Angeles Times,* Edwin Schallert kept things in a holiday mood in his review:

Ernst Lubitsch, with a harlequin air, again kicks up a rumpus in the cream-puff kingdoms. With monkey business—raucous, riotous, racy and occasionally even raw—he turns the pageantry of monarchs into a holiday of zanyism and buffoonery . . . I like this type of Lubitsch devilment. I like the elements of surprise in his humor.

And, in the *Los Angeles Examiner,* Jerry Hoffman said:

The Smiling Lieutenant is more Lubitsch than any character in it. One sees the intense, directorial Lubitsch, projecting through Chevalier, a subconscious Lubitsch, the actor. Ere this bring the wrath of Chevalier's followers on my head—of course there is Chevalier! The Chevalier! The One Chevalier! There is no argument about his personality nor yet his ability. Even when he does sing off-key, for Maurice, this is the nearest to *The Love Parade* movie producers have given him.

With Miriam Hopkins

ONE HOUR WITH YOU

A PARAMOUNT PICTURE 1932

With Jeanette MacDonald

With Genevieve Tobin

With Lili Damita (French version)

With Genevieve Tobin

With Jeanette MacDonald

Produced by Ernst Lubitsch. Directed by Ernst Lubitsch and George Cukor. Screenplay by Samson Raphaelson. Based on the play, "Nur ein Traum, Luctspiel in 3 Akten," by Lothar Schmidt (Goldschmidt). Photographed by Victor Milner. Art Direction Supervised by Hans Dreier. Set Decoration Supervision by A. E. Freudeman. Music and Lyrics by Oscar Straus, Richard A. Whiting and Leo Robin. Musical Arrangements and Orchestrations by the Paramount Music Department under the supervision of Nathaniel W. Finston. Sound Recording by Western Electric. Sound Engineer, M. M. Paggie. Gowns by Travis Banton. Film Cutter, William Shea. Filmed in Hollywood. 80 minutes.

SONGS:

"What Would You Do?," "Oh, That Mitzi!," "What A Little Thing Like a Wedding Ring Can Do" and "Three Times a Day" sung by Maurice Chevalier. "It Was Only a Dream Kiss" sung by Jeanette MacDonald. "We Will Always Be Sweethearts" sung by Chevalier and MacDonald. "One Hour with You" sung by Chevalier, MacDonald and cast members.

CAST:

Dr. André Bertier, MAURICE CHEVALIER; *Colette Bertier,* JEANETTE MacDONALD; *Mitzi Olivier,* GENEVIEVE TOBIN; *Professor Olivier,* Roland YOUNG; *Adolph,* Charles RUGGLES; *Police Commissioner,* George Barbier; *Mlle. Martel,* Josephine Dunn; *Detective,* Richard Carle; *Policeman,* Charles Judels; *Mitzi's Maid,* Barbara Leonard; *Marcel,* Charles C. Coleman; *Colette's Downstairs Maid,* Sheila Mannors; *Colette's Upstairs Maid,* Leonie Pray; *Taxi Driver,* George David.

STORY:

Dr. André Bertier chances to meet the flirtatious Mitzi Olivier, who encourages an affair although she is the best friend of André's wife, Colette.

When a private detective he has hired gives Professor Olivier a full report on his wife's indiscretions, he tells Dr. Bertier he intends filing for divorce and naming him co-respondent. When Colette hears of this, from her husband's lips, she's crushed at first but soon retaliates by allowing a family friend and ardent admirer, Adolph, to make love to her.

Having proved to André that two can play the same game, Colette dismisses Adolph and suggests to her husband that they settle down. Relieved to have his wife's affections again, and to be extricated from a scandal, André promises he'll never stray again.

UNE HEURE PRÈS DE TOI

Paramount's French-language version of *One Hour with You,* directed by Ernst Lubitsch, with a French language screenplay and song lyrics translated by Leopold Marchand and André Hornez. With the exceptions of Genevieve Tobin, Roland Young, Charles Ruggles and George Barbier (replaced, respectively, by Lily Damita, Ernest Ferny, Pierre Etchepare and André Cheron), the cast was the same as in the English language version. 80 minutes.

With Jeanette MacDonald

COMMENTS AND CRITIQUES:

Maurice Chevalier's third film for director Ernst Lubitsch, a remake of Lubitsch's 1924 Warner Brothers film *The Marriage Circle* (which starred Florence Vidor, Monte Blue, Marie Prevost, Creighton Hale and Adolphe Menjou) was an assignment he had been reluctant to accept. It was only after script revisions he demanded were completed and he was assured that Carole Lombard, for whom he had a great admiration, and Kay Francis, with whom he was romantically involved, would be his leading ladies did he agree to do it. Then, just before production began, Lombard and Francis, because of other commitments, were replaced by Jeanette MacDonald, whom Lubitsch had wanted in the first place, and Genevieve Tobin. Soon after that Lubitsch, who had not completed his direction of *Broken Lullaby,* was made overall production supervisor of Paramount films. These changes of studio policy necessitated assigning George Cukor to direct *One Hour with You.*

Midway in production, when Lubitsch had the time to devote his attention to *One Hour with You,* he began making suggestions to Cukor. A thoroughly capable and creative director in his own right, Cukor felt it was no longer his film and abdicated to Lubitsch. He then had to arbitrate Paramount's intention of giving Lubitsch solo directorial credit until a compromise resulted in his name being included on the credits and advertisements. By this time the film was already in release and critics were praising Lubitsch!

The most important organ in show business, *Weekly Variety,* said:

A money picture—Chevalier practically insures that—even if the screen treatment is a bit radical and may be open to debate as to how the hinterland will accept its unorthodox presentation. But it's a 100% credit to all concerned, principally Ernst Lubitsch on his production and direction, which required no little courage to carry out the continuity idea.

The unorthodoxy concerns Chevalier's interpolated, confidential asides to his audience, in the *Strange Interlude* manner, although in an altogether gay spirit. Chevalier periodically interrupts the romantic sequence to come downscreen for a close-up to intimately address the "ladies and gentlemen" as to his amorous problems.

In *The New York Times,* Mordaunt Hall said:

Through the connivance of Adolph Zukor and Ernst Lubitsch, Maurice Chevalier's prepossessing shadow was presented last night in a picture reveling in the title of *One Hour with You* at both the Rivoli and the Rialto. If the gathering in the latter theatre laughed as much as that in the former house, then it was a jolly hour or so in the two places.

The latest Lubitsch production, aided by M. Chevalier and his supporting cast, is filled with scintillating wit of the Paris variety . . . M. Chevalier is as enjoyable as ever. There is his smile and also his stare—a stare of discomfort when he is dumbfounded. But whether he is solemn or laughing, he is always engaging . . . *One Hour with You* is an excellent production, with Lubitsch and Chevalier at the top of their form.

In the *Los Angeles Times,* Edwin Schallert said:

The Lubitsch *touch,* which has become more than a legend, is omnipresent in this production and Chevalier's comedy is, as usual, dependable. He has a great flair for evoking the surprise. And his pantomine, as well as his words, always seems sure fire. Vive la France! Also Vive M. le Chevalier and Ernst Lubitsch!

After the French version, *Une Heure Près de Toi,* opened in Paris, *Weekly Variety* acknowledged the occasion with a brief review, signed by "Maxi":

The Chevalier-MacDonald combination, with Lily Damita—also popular—thrown in, cannot fail to draw, but French audiences find that there is nothing to the film. To their taste it is slow and without punch.

With Jeanette MacDonald, Genevieve Tobin and Roland Young

A PARAMOUNT PICTURE 1932

Chevalier played himself in a cameo appearance

Produced by Louis D. Lighton. Directed by William Beaudine. Screenplay by Sam Mintz, Walter DeLeon and Arthur Kober. Based on the novel, "Merton of the Movies," by Harry Leon Wilson and the play by George S. Kaufman and Marc Connelly. Photographed by Allan Siegler. Sound Recording by Western Electric. Sound Engineer, Earle S. Hayman. Edited by LeRoy Stone. Filmed in Hollywood. 83 minutes.

CAST:

Merton Gill, STUART ERWIN; *"Flips" Montague,* JOAN BLONDELL; *Mrs. Scudder,* ZaSu PITTS; *Himself,* Ben TURPIN; *Mr. Gashwiler,* Charles Sellon; *Mrs. Gashwiler,* Florence Roberts; *Tessie Kearns,* Helen Jerome Eddy; *Hardy Powell,* Arthur Hoyt; *Buck Benson,* George Templeton; *The Countess,* Ruth Donnelly; *Jeff Baird,* Sam Hardy; *Henshaw,* Oscar Apfel; *Ma Patterson,* Katherine Clare Ward; *Chuck Collins,* Frank Mills; *Doris Randall,* Polly Walters; *Fellow Actors:* Victor Potel, Bobby Vernon, Snub Pollard, Billy Bletcher, Bud Jamison, Nick Thompson.

GUEST STARS *(as Themselves):*

TALLULAH BANKHEAD; CLIVE BROOK; MAURICE CHEVALIER; CLAUDETTE COLBERT; GARY COOPER; PHILLIPS HOLMES; FREDRIC MARCH; JACK OAKIE; CHARLES RUGGLES; SYLVIA SIDNEY.

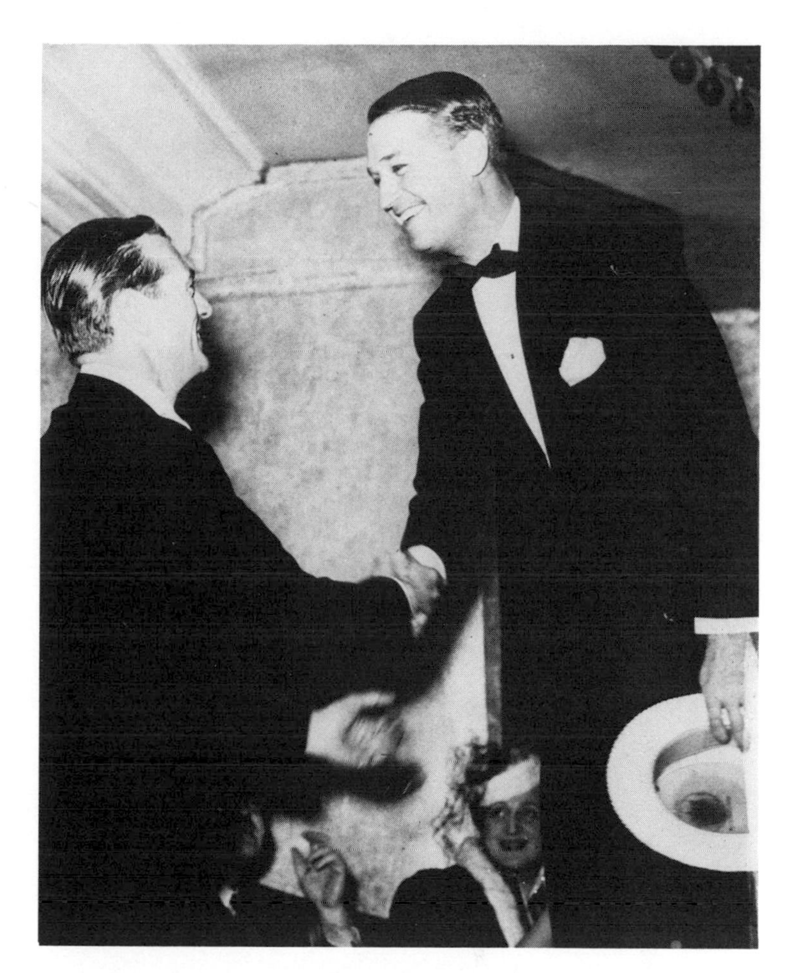

With Gary Cooper at the Hollywood première

COMMENTS AND CRITIQUES:

The first sound version of *Merton of the Movies* (it had been made by Paramount in 1924 with Glenn Hunter and was made again in 1947 by MGM with Red Skelton) included glimpses of famous Paramount players, as themselves, involved in the fictional plot concerned with Merton Gill's attempts to become a film star. Maurice Chevalier, coming from the set of *Love Me Tonight,* stops to chat with Merton and suggests he tilt his cowboy hat to the same rakish angle he wears his straw hat.

In the *Los Angeles Times,* Philip K. Scheuer, said:

Studio scenes, which provide glimpses of Maurice Chevalier and other Paramount people—"informally," of course, are treated without exaggeration. The whole production, indeed, has been handled with intelligence and rare sympathy by Director William Beaudine.

Joan Blondell and Stuart Erwin

LOVE ME TONIGHT
A PARAMOUNT PICTURE 1932

Produced and Directed by Rouben Mamoulian. Screenplay by Samuel Hoffenstein, Waldemar Young and George Marion, Jr.; based on a play, "Tailor in the Chateau," by Leopold Marchand and Paul Armont. Photographed by Victor Milner. Art Direction by Hans Dreier. Sets by A. E. Freudeman. Costumes designed and supervised by Travis Banton. Music and lyrics by Richard Rodgers and Lorenz Hart. Orchestral Arrangements and Musical Supervision by the Paramount Music Department under the direction of Nathaniel Finston. Sound Recording by M. M. Paggie. Film Cutter: Billy Shea. Filmed in Hollywood. 105 minutes.

Rouben Mamoulian directing Chevalier

SONGS:

"The Song of Paree," "How Are You?" and "Poor Apache" sung by Maurice Chevalier. "Lover" sung by Jeanette MacDonald. "Love Me Tonight" and "Isn't It Romantic?" sung by Chevalier-MacDonald (reprise of latter sung by Bert Roach, Rolf Sedan and Tyler Brooke). "A Woman Needs Something Like That" sung by MacDonald and Joseph Cawthorn. "Mimi" sung by Chevalier, with Myrna Loy, C. Aubrey Smith, Charles Ruggles, Charles Butterworth, Elizabeth Patterson, Ethel Griffies and Blanche Friderici. "The Son of a Gun is Nothing But a Tailor" sung by supporting cast principals.

CAST:

Maurice Courtelin, MAURICE CHEVALIER; *Princess Jeanette,* JEANETTE MacDONALD; *Gilbert, Vicomte de Vareze,* Charles RUGGLES; *Count de Savignac,* Charles BUTTERWORTH; *Countess Valentine,* Myrna LOY; *The Duke d'Artelines,* C. Aubrey SMITH; *First Aunt,* Elizabeth Patterson; *Second Aunt,* Ethel Griffies; *Third Aunt,* Blanche Friderici; *The Doctor,* Joseph Cawthorn; *Major-Domo,* Robert Grieg; *Dressmaker,* Ethel Wales; *Bakery Girl,* Marion "Peanuts" Byron; *Mme. Dupont,* Mary Doran; *Emile,* Bert Roach; *Laundress,* Cecil Cunningham; *Composer,* Tyler Brooke; *Valet,* Edgar Norton; *Groom,* Herbert Mundin; *Chambermaid,* Rita Owin; *Shirtmaker,* Clarence Wilson; *Collector,* Gordon Westcott; *Pierre,* George Davis; *Taxi Driver,* Rolf Sedan; *Hat Maker,* Tony Merle; *Boot Maker,* William H. Turner; *Grocer,* George "Gabby" Hayes; *Chef,* George Humbert.

With Jeanette MacDonald

STORY:

After making sixteen suits for the Vicomte de Vareze and then lending him a few hundred francs,

Maurice Courtelin, "the best tailor in all France," discovers that the nobleman, surprised by an irate husband whose wife was extending her favors to him, has fled Paris and retreated to his country chateau. Learning, too, that his credit rating is zero, Maurice follows in hot pursuit. Enroute he encounters the beautiful but haughty Princess Jeanette who, he soon discovers, also lives at the chateau.

Alarmed by the tailor's arrival, the Vicomte, who will be disfavored by his uncle, The Duke, if his predicament is discovered, introduces Maurice as a baron. In that guise he ultimately charms every member of the household, especially the three maiden aunts and the Countess Valentine who are the attendant chaperones of Princess Jeanette.

Everyone is aghast when his masquerade is discovered and a sick-at-heart Maurice boards a train for Paris. But Princess Jeanette, realizing she loves him, pursues the train on horseback and forces it to stop. The lovers embrace as the scene then dissolves back to the chateau where the three maiden aunts sing their approval.

COMMENTS AND CRITIQUES:

Like vintage champagne, *Love Me Tonight*, 1932's most perfect film, improves with age and its screening at film retrospectives is always the event most anticipated and acclaimed. And no discerning film student or scholar disputes the word-of-mouth acclaim which now justly decrees it the all-time best screen musical.

Conforming to no previously established pattern in the genre, the sparkle, spontaneity and exquisite pleasures of *Love Me Tonight* are more potent than ever. Critically acclaimed, and moderately successful when first released, it had its greatest popularity in Europe, notably France, where some of the more risqué lyrics of its songs, Myrna Loy's reprise of "Mimi," sung while wearing a very revealing negligee, and "A Woman Needs Something Like That," a sophisticated tribute to the benisons of physical sex, were not excised as they had been from the version exhibited for general release in the U.S.

In his contemporary review in *The New York Times*, Mordaunt Hall said:

Mr. Mamoulian is at the height of his form and never neglects an opportunity to conjure with the microphone or make the most of the camera.

And, in the *Los Angeles Times*, Philip K. Scheuer said:

It has, for me, the sort of magic which makes the theater, the screen, that rarest of places, a refuge from a troubled world. It is, in substance, a picture I would like to take home with me, so that on dull evenings I could bring it out and display it to my friends, and make them happy too.

Really a stylized fairy tale, *Love Me Tonight* is a stunning example of co-ordination in the making of a musical movie. Excellently cast, kinetically photographed, flawlessly mounted, it rejoices additionally in a synchronic score which punctuates the flow of the gay comedy and lends a final fillip to each camera sentence.

In the *Los Angeles Examiner*, Jerry Hoffman stated:

It's one of the best, if not the very best of the Maurice Chevalier pictures—and not the least of the cause is the brilliant direction by Rouben Mamoulian.

Some thirty-five years after its original release, John Baxter, in his book, "Hollywood in the Thirties," declared:

If there is a better musical of the Thirties, one wonders what it can be.

In the course of discussing *Love Me Tonight* with Rouben Mamoulian at his home one afternoon, he told the authors this:

One day shortly after I finished *Dr. Jekyll and Mr. Hyde*, and everybody was happy about its prospects, I encountered Adolph Zukor on the lot. As you know, the executives of this era were often far more persuasive actors than the players under contract to them. Zukor, with tears in his eyes, implored me to produce and direct a film with Maurice Chevalier and Jeanette MacDonald. Both of them were under big salaried contracts to Paramount and, according to Zukor, the studio was on the brink of bankruptcy so it was imperative that stars like Chevalier and MacDonald be constantly used. I protested that I wasn't the man for the job, that Lubitsch had done very well with these two players in the past, and suggested Mr. Zukor approach him. But Lubitsch was busy with other projects, Zukor said, and wouldn't I please give it a try?

I promised to think about it, and the more I thought about it, the more interesting doing a light musical film became to me. But I couldn't find a suitable property. And then at a party, while talking to Leopold Marchand, a European writer then working at Paramount, I learned

Chevalier doing his "I'm an Apache" number

that he had a slight story idea that might be attractive. It was only two pages long, but when I read it, I thought it had a kind of fairy tale romantic magic, and I asked the studio to buy it.

I then got Richard Rodgers and Lorenz Hart to develop the songs for the film. You understand, all the songs were carefully planned, with the lyrics to advance the story line, and their place in the story itself designed before the writers of the screenplay were engaged. This is the way an original musical film should be developed, in my opinion, but it so seldom happens like this. When the screenwriters—Hoffenstein, Marion Jr., and Young—came on the picture it was their job to construct the scenes and bridge the dialog between the song numbers, so that the songs flowed from the action sequences and the actors didn't stop and sing a song. It worked perfectly.

Only Chevalier was, in the beginning, disturbed. He approached me one day and said, "I understand you're having story conferences on my next picture." I told him yes, that was true, but I was first working with the song writers. He wondered why he wasn't included in the discussions. Lubitsch, he said, always had him

Left to right: C. Aubrey Smith, Charles Ruggles, Chevalier, Myrna Loy, Jeanette MacDonald, Charles Butterworth, Elizabeth Patterson, Blanche Friderici, Ethel Griffies

present at all pre-production meetings. I said that was all very well; that was the way Lubitsch worked; but Lubitsch wasn't doing *Love Me Tonight*—I was, and I worked my way, and I especially didn't want him on hand at story conferences. He was hurt and said he would complain to the front office. I told him to please do so, that I hadn't wanted to do this picture and was only doing it as a great favor to Mr. Zukor, and would consider it a very special favor if he could get me taken off it.

Maurice, of course, didn't go to the front office. He loved the script when it was shown to him, and was enchanted by all the Rodgers and Hart songs. *Love Me Tonight* turned out to be one of my happiest film productions, and I was delighted that it met with such critical and public favor when it was released. I'm even more pleased that now, *over forty years later,* young audiences in cinema classes and film groups are so entertained by it and that film critics all over the world, on judging it anew, hold it in such high esteem that it gets even better notices than it did originally.

And, of course, making *Love Me Tonight* brought me together with Maurice Chevalier—and we remained close friends all his life. That I especially cherish.

With Myrna Loy and Jeanette MacDonald

With Jeanette MacDonald

A BEDTIME STORY

A PARAMOUNT PICTURE 1933

With Helen Twelvetrees

An Emanuel Cohen Production. Directed by Norman Taurog. Screenplay by Waldemar Young. Adapted by Benjamin Glazer, from the novel, "Bellamy the Magnificent," by Roy Horniman. Photographed by Charles Lang. Music and Lyrics by Ralph Rainger and Leo Robin. Orchestrations and Arrangements by the Paramount Music Department, under the supervision of Nathaniel W. Finston. Sound Recording by Western Electric. Chief Sound Engineer, Franklin Hansen. Gowns by Travis Banton. Edited by Otto Lovering. Filmed in Hollywood. 85 minutes.

With Edward Everett Horton

SONGS:

"M'sieu Baby," "In a Park in Paree," "Look What I've Got" and "Home-Made Heaven," sung by Maurice Chevalier.

CAST:

René, Vicomte de St. Denis, MAURICE CHEVALIER; *Sally,* HELEN TWELVETREES; *Victor,* Edward Everett HORTON; *Paulette,* Adrienne Ames; *"Monsieur,"* Baby Leroy; *Max,* Earle Foxe; *Suzanne,* Betty Lorraine; *Louise,* Gertrude Michael; *Robert,* Ernest Wood; *General,* Reginald Mason; *Agent de Police,* Henry Kolker; *Henry Joudain,* George MacQuarrie; *Concierge,* Paul Panzer.

With Leah Ray and Adrienne Ames

STORY:

Returning unexpectedly to Paris after big game hunting in Africa for a year, René, Vicomte de St. Denis, discovers his fiancée, Louise, committed to a social obligation she can't break. Finding himself free he arranges dates with his old flames, Paulette, Gabrielle and Suzanne, at precisely timed assignations. But when a baby boy, abandoned by his destitute parents, is discovered in René's limousine, his plans for a night of *l'amour d'oeuvre* are cancelled. Infuriated at first by this circumstance, René ultimately succumbs to the infant's charms and decides to adopt him.

He engages Sally, an unemployed vaudevillian stranded in Paris, as nursemaid for "M'sieu Baby" and rearranges his own living habits to the child's well being. He later takes the baby with him to a party at his fiancée's home where the guests present believe him to be the father. Intimidated, Louise breaks her engagement and returns René his ring thinking this will bring him to his senses

With Helen Twelvetrees and Baby Leroy

With Edward Everett Horton and Baby Leroy

Chevalier and Baby Leroy between scenes

and he'll turn the baby over to the authorities to place in an orphanage.

Instead, René, relieved to be free of Louise, patches up his misunderstanding with Sally and gives her the engagement ring, realizing how much he and "M'sieu Baby" love and need her.

COMMENTS AND CRITIQUES:

A Bedtime Story was neither novel in story concept nor especially captivating in execution. The idea of the least likely person possible suddenly finding himself deferring his routine to a child's needs and temperaments had been explored in films, before and since, with much more satisfying results. What did make this film unique, aside from Maurice Chevalier's incandescent charm, was the uncanny performance of six-month-old Ronald Leroy Overacker, better known as Baby Leroy, who achieved overnight stardom and, for several years, played important roles in other Paramount films: *Design For Living, Tillie and Gus, Torch Singer, Miss Fane's Baby is Stolen, The Lemon Drop Kid, It's A Gift, The Old-Fashioned Way* and *It's A Great Life.* Retired before he was four years old, Baby Leroy made one abortive attempt at a film comeback (in 1940) before returning to obscurity. But during his forty-month reign at Paramount, he contributed his share to the legends of Hollywood in the 1930's. Maurice Chevalier offered to adopt him (his parents were separated) and Mae West promised to give him her undivided attention when he was old enough to come 'n' see her. Because of his ability to upstage and steal scenes with ease, several stars declined working with him. His most constant co-star, W. C. Fields, got him drunk on one occasion and withered aghast co-workers with his famous "Any man who hates dogs and children can't be all bad" attitude by exclaiming, "The boy's no trouper. Anyone who can't hold his liquor shouldn't drink on the job."

Moderately popular with audiences at the time of its release, *A Bedtime Story* was one of a large bloc of old Paramount films reissued in 1949. But public reaction to it was not intense enough for them to do a remake of it with Bob Hope as they had originally planned.

And contemporary critics were only mildly enthusiastic. In the *Los Angeles Times,* Philip K. Scheuer said:

Constructed along lines which are at once practical and intimate, *A Bedtime Story* is geared at low speed throughout—a change from the brisk tempos of Chevalier's earlier vehicles, made under the management of Messrs. Lubitsch and Mamoulian. It is as different from, for instance, his most recent, brilliant *Love Me Tonight* as may be imagined, and is less a fantasy or a farce than it is a strictly conventional photographed comedy. As such it will find most favor with those who prefer a picture that takes its time, particularly when it is strewn with lengthy close-ups of such a nursling as Baby Leroy, in action, and in repose . . . *A Bedtime Story* is undistinguished but ingratiating. Chevalier at his mildest.

In the *Los Angeles Examiner,* Louella Parsons said:

The charming Maurice Chevalier and a baby are all any woman needs to make her day complete . . . *A Bedtime Story* will do much for him with his fans. It is just what every woman will enjoy seeing, a charming, simple and really amusing picture. Chevalier's lullabies (he sings two) are even more delightful than his love lyrics.

In the New York *Times,* Mordaunt Hall said:

By periodical outbursts of crying, occasional smiles and the babbling of something that sounds like Da-da or Da-di-da, an infant designated on the program as Baby Leroy gives a performance that rivals in interest that of Maurice Chevalier in the film, *A Bedtime Story* . . . The producers are already looking around for another narrative in which to cast this speechless prodigy.

With Ethel Wales and Frank Reicher

A PARAMOUNT PICTURE 1933

With Jacqueline Francelle in the French language version

Produced by Benjamin Glazer. Directed by Norman Taurog. Screenplay by Gene Fowler and Benjamin Glazer, adapted from their original story, "Laughing Man." Additional dialog by Claude Binyon and Frank Butler. Photographed by Charles Lang. Music and Lyrics by Ralph Rainger and Leo Robin. Orchestrations and Arrangements by the Paramount Music Department under the supervision of Nathaniel W. Finston. Sound Recording by Western Electric. Chief Sound Engineer, Franklin Hansen. Art Direction Supervised by Hans Dreier. Film Cutter, William Shea. Filmed in Hollywood. 80 minutes.

SONGS:

"Lucky Guy," "Lover of Paree" and "In a One-Room Flat," sung by Maurice Chevalier.

CAST:

François, MAURICE CHEVALIER; *Madeleine,* ANN DVORAK; *Professor Gaston Bibi,* Edward Everett HORTON; *Monsieur Joe,* Arthur Pierson; *Suzanne,* Minna Gombell; *Rosalie,* Blanche Friderici; *Agent Chapusard,* Douglass Dumbrille; *Marco,* John Miljan; *Pierre,* Sidney Toler; *Wladek, the Mighty,* George Hagen; *Pedro,* George Rigas; *Anna-Marie,* Nydia Westman; *Monsieur Prial,* Billy Bevan; *Guide,* Jason Robards, Sr., *A Sunburned Lady,* Grace Bradley; *A Drunk,* Arthur Housman; *Casanova, a Dog,* Mutt.

STORY:

While waiting to take an examination qualifying him to work as an official Paris tourist guide, which will fulfill a lifetime ambition, François works temporarily as a sidewalk hawker by wearing a sign bearing the legend "Is Your Heart Happy? No? Consult Professor Bibi, 17 Rue Canton." His one occupational hazard is tactfully repelling the advances of Professor Bibi's hot-blooded niece, Anna-Marie, who thinks he'll make her an ideal husband.

In the course of eluding the altar-eager Anna-Marie, François rescues a dog from impoundment and helps a beautiful girl, Madeleine, elude her carnival act partner, Pedro, a jealous knife-thrower.

After passing his test and becoming a guide, François proposes to Madeleine, but Anna-Marie, with whom she has been staying, tells her she is unworthy of being his wife. Unaware that Anna-Marie has her own motives, Madeleine rejects his offer and returns to the carnival as the human target in Pedro's knife-throwing exhibition. There, after a drunken spree, and an encounter with a professional wrestler, François again rescues Madeleine from Pedro and finally persuades her to marry him.

L'AMOUR GUIDE

Paramount's filmed-in-Hollywood French-language version of *The Way to Love,* co-directed by Norman Taurog and Gil Pratt, with dialog translated by Jean Boyer and song lyrics translated by Andre Hornez. Maurice Chevalier repeated his role as *François* and other members of the cast included Jacqueline Francelle, Marcel Vallée, Adrienne d'Ambricourt, Emile Chautard, Germaine de Neel, Bruce Wyndham, Leonie Pray, George Hagen and Georges Renavent. 80 minutes.

COMMENTS AND CRITIQUES:

The Way to Love, Maurice Chevalier's last film under his Paramount contract, was plagued with production problems. Two and a half weeks after filming commenced on the English language version, Sylvia Sidney, cast in the role of *Madeleine,* walked off the picture claiming to be seriously ill. Paramount felt she was merely trying to get out of a mediocre assignment, but doctors upheld her claim. Carole Lombard was called in to replace her, but after reading the script she balked and said she would rather go on suspension than do the film. After that no contract player on the Paramount lot was approachable about accepting the part and production was held up until Ann Dvorak, on loan-out from Warner Brothers, came to the rescue. By then several members of the original supporting cast, including Kathleen Burke, were committed to other assignments and all footage already shot, except for a scene involving Chevalier, Douglass Dumbrille and Mutt, the dog, had to be scuttled.

While all this was going on, Paramount was fruitlessly attempting to negotiate a new contract with Chevalier and hoping to keep him working under their trademark. But the studio, on the verge of bankruptcy and almost at the point of putting their assets in the hands of receivers, were unable to equal the attractive offer Chevalier had received from Irving Thalberg at MGM. Already shorthanded of stars, because of Myron Selznick's famous "talent-raid" six months earlier (when he took over the management of three of their biggest

With Ann Dvorak

From the French-language version

With Adrienne d'Ambricourt and Marcel Vallee in the French language version

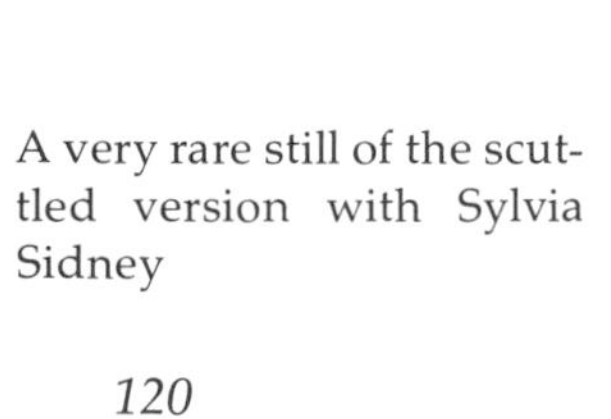

A very rare still of the scuttled version with Sylvia Sidney

names, Ruth Chatterton, William Powell and Kay Francis, and successfully bargained lucrative new contracts for them at Warner Brothers while they had been waiting for Paramount to pick up their options), Paramount, financially strapped (and unaware that Mae West's *She Done Him Wrong* would soon pull them out of the red), was loath to let Chevalier go and was momentarily stymied.

Chevalier, on the other hand, had not been happy with his last two films, and since no property offered him as a subsequent vehicle looked any more promising, he elected to accept the MGM offer. He later said that if Paramount had found a film for him to do with either Marlene Dietrich, Carole Lombard or Mae West he would have signed up with them for life.

Most trade paper reviews of *The Way to Love* merely echoed the sentiments of *Weekly Variety:*

The poorest of the Chevaliers, but fair entertainment which will get by on the strength of the star. Will need all his marquee support. Ann Dvorak is the lead in the role on which Sylvia Sidney walked out and it becomes evident why a full-fledged star would balk at the relatively stooge assignment . . . Chevalier, seemingly conscious of yeoman needs to impress, works his personality overtime and to good effect, particularly in the song numbers.

In *The New York Times,* Mordaunt Hall, a confirmed Chevalier fan, said:

M. Chevalier, usually wearing his familiar straw hat, sings delightfully and he makes Francois a thoroughly ingratiating vagabond.

With Ann Dvorak and George Rigas

With Douglass Dumbrille and Mutt

A METRO-GOLDWYN-MAYER PICTURE 1934

With Jeanette MacDonald

*Executive Producer, Irving Thalberg. Associate Producer and Director, Ernst Lubitsch. Screenplay by Ernest Vajda and Samson Raphaelson. Based on Franz Lehar's operetta, "The Merry Widow," Libretto and Lyrics by Victor Leon and Leo Stein. Photographed by Oliver T. Marsh. Music by Franz Lehar. Additional Music by Richard Rodgers. Lyrics by Lorenz Hart and Gus Kahn. Music Adapted, Arranged, Orchestrated and Conducted by Herbert Stothart. Sound Recording Engineer, Douglas Shearer. Art Direction and Set Decoration by Cedric Gibbons, Gabriel Scognamillo, Fredric Hope and Edwin B. Willis. Choreography by Albertina Rasch. Gowns by Adrian. Men's Costumes by Ali Hubert. Edited by Frances Marsh. Filmed at MGM's Culver City studio. 110 minutes**

SONGS:

"Girls, Girls, Girls," "Widows Are Gay," "I'm Going to Maxime's" sung by Maurice Chevalier. "Vilia" and "Tonight Will Teach Me to Forget" sung by Jeanette MacDonald. "Melody of Laughter" (instrumental). "The Merry Widow Waltz" sung by Chevalier and MacDonald.

CAST:

Danilo, MAURICE CHEVALIER; *Sonia,* JEANETTE MacDONALD; *Ambassador,* Edward Everett HORTON; *Queen,* Una Merkel; *King,* George Barbier; *Marcele,* Minna Gombell; *Lulu,* Ruth Channing; *Orderly,* Sterling Holloway; *Turk,* Henry Armetta; *Maid,* Barbara Leonard; *Valet,* Donald Meek; *Manager of Maxime's,* Akim Tamiroff; *Zizipoff,* Herman Bing; *Adamovitch,* Lucien Prival; *Sonia's Maids:* Luana Walters, Sheila Mannors, Caryl Lincoln, Edna Waldron, Lona Andre; *Maxime's Girls:* Patricia Farley, Shirley Chambers (Ross), Maria Troubetskoy, Eleanor Hunt, Jean Hart, Dorothy Wilson, Barbara Barondess, Dorothy Granger, Jill Bennett, Mary Jane Halsey, Peggy Watts, Dorothy Dehn and Connie Lamont; *Escorts,* Charles Requa, George Lewis, Tyler Brooke, John Merkyl and Cosmo Kyrle Bellew; *Policemen:* Roger Gray, Christian J. Frank, Otto Fries, George Magrill and John Roach; *Waiters:* Gino Corrado and Perry Ivins; *Prisoner,* Kathleen Burke; *Ambassador,* George Baxter; *Dancer,* Paul Ellis; *Shepherd,* Leonid Kinskey; *Newspaper Woman,* Evelyn Selbie; *Lackey,* Wedg-

*The English language reissue version of *The Merry Widow,* available for national bookings since 1962 as one of the MGM "Golden Operetta" series, runs 103 minutes.

With Jeanette MacDonald

With Edward Everett Horton in the French-language version

wood Nowell; *Defense Attorney,* Richard Carle; *Prosecuting Attorney,* Morgan Wallace; *Judge,* Frank Sheridan; *Doorman,* Arthur Byron; *Wardrobe Mistress,* Claudia Coleman; *Excited Chinaman,* Lee Tin; *Animal Woman,* Nora Cecil; *Orthodox Priest,* Tom Frances; *Nondescript Priest,* Winter Hall; *Newsboy,* Matty Rupert; *Fat Lackeys:* Dewey Robinson, Russell Powell and Billy Gilbert; *Drunks,* Arthur Housman and Johnny "Skins" Miller; *Gypsy Leader,* Hector Sarno; *Violinist,* Jan Rubini; *Arresting Officer,* Jason Robards, Sr.; *Headwaiter,* Albert Pollet; *Gabrielovitsch,* Rolf Sedan; *Goatman,* Jacques Lory.

STORY:

When the beautiful widow Sonia departs from the kingdom of Marshovia for Paris, the King is alarmed. She controls 52 percent of the country's wealth and its financial security depends on her spending it there. Discovering the roguish Prince Danilo in the Queen's boudoir, the King banishes him to Paris with instructions to win the widow's heart and return her to Marshovia—or face the consequences of a court-martial.

Once in Paris, Danilo encounters Sonia at Maxime's, where she is pretending to be one of the gay cabaret girls. Although they dance together, and Danilo falls in love with her, they soon part, neither aware of the other's true identity.

They meet again, at an embassy ball in Marshovia, and Sonia learns Danilo's identity and the nature of his mission to Paris. Threatening to leave the country permanently, she remains long enough to testify at Danilo's court-martial that he did everything possible to woo her. Nevertheless, Danilo is convicted. Inveigled into visiting him in his cell, Sonia, on orders from the King, is locked up with Danilo until she agrees to marry him.

LA VEUVE JOYEUSE

MGM's simultaneously produced French language version of *The Merry Widow,* directed by Ernst Lubitsch from a screenplay translated by Marcel Achard with French lyrics by André Hornez. Maurice Chevalier and Jeanette MacDonald recreated their roles but in this version Akim Tamiroff played *Turk.* Other cast members included Marcel Vallée, Mme. Daniele Parola, André Berley, Fifi D'Orsay, Pauline Garon, George Davis, Jean Perry, Albert Petit, Emil Dellys, Georges Renavent, Georgette Rhodes, Anita Pike, Odette Duval, Lya

Lys, George Nardelli, Constant Franke, Jacques Venaire, George Renault, Marcel Ventura, Fred Cravens, Sam Ash, Harry Lamont, George de Gombert, Arthur de Ravenne, Fred Malatesta, George Colega, Adrienne d'Ambricourt, Eugene Borden, Jules Raucourt, André Cheron, Eugene Beday, Juliet Dika, Carry Daumery, August Tollaire, Gene Gouldeni, Jacques Lory, André Ferrier. 114 minutes.

COMMENTS AND CRITIQUES:

The contract Maurice Chevalier signed with MGM gave him script approval, time off for stage appearances and the right to make "outside" films. In addition to this lavish remake of *The Merry Widow*, MGM had three subsequent properties they were readying which had Chevalier's approval: *The Chocolate Soldier*, a musical version of *The Last of Mrs. Cheyney* and a charming romantic comedy, *Escapade*.

The first note of dissention in this potential paradise occurred when Irving Thalberg rejected Chevalier's suggestion that Grace Moore be cast as *The Merry Widow.* Thalberg's reluctance to comply was not without foundation. Four years earlier Miss Moore had starred in two costly MGM failures, *A Lady's Morals* and *New Moon*, which convinced him she had no screen potential. But late in 1935, after Miss Moore's triumphant return to the screen in Columbia's *One Night of Love*, MGM offered to borrow her to co-star with Chevalier in *The Chocolate Soldier*—but when Miss Moore specified she had to receive top-billing, Chevalier declined. At a professional impasse, he announced he was returning to France—permanently. By mutual agreement, his MGM contract was cancelled.

One of his reasons for suggesting Grace Moore was Chevalier's reluctance to co-star with Jeanette MacDonald, whom MGM was promoting—in their three Paramount films Miss MacDonald was only featured. He considered her elevation to stardom in his film an admission that his solo star status had declined. And although he had a great professional admiration for Miss MacDonald's beauty and talent, he personally regarded her as something of a prude. And he felt that her puritanical attitude was something of an affectation since he had been a first-hand witness to her stormy romance with talent agent Bob Ritchie while they were under contract to Paramount. And Chevalier, as did many

Ernst Lubitsch directing Chevalier and Jeanette MacDonald

With Jeanette MacDonald

With the Can-Can girls

others, believed Miss MacDonald had been secretly married to Ritchie but had had the marriage annulled in Paris shortly before signing with MGM. Discussing Chevalier many years afterward, Miss MacDonald, is a moment of unusual (for her) candor, referred to him as "The fastest *derrière* pincher in Hollywood."

None of these feelings, however, came through on the screen. *The Merry Widow* was a sparkling, romantic and lushly mounted production that eschewed the sexual fetishes and eroticisms which made Erich von Stroheim's 1925 version such a curiously uneven film. And MGM's sumptuous Technicolor version, made in 1952, starred a glamorously turned-out, somewhat miscast, Lana Turner in a role which required her to sing, dance

and play sophisticated comedy. None of which was exactly her *forte*.

Of the Lubitsch version, André Sennwald, in *The New York Times*, said:

It is a good show in the excellent Lubitsch manner, heady as the foam on champagne, fragile as mist and as delicately gay as the good-natured censor will permit. . . . Although some of the ensemble numbers, particularly the embassy ball, are breathtaking, Herr Lubitsch is not the man to crush you under a mountain of spectacle. His sense of humor is impeccable and his taste is faultless. So with his actors. There was an inconsiderate rumor not long ago that Mr. Chevalier was diminishing

With Daniele Parola and Andre Berley (French-language version)

With Fifi D'Orsay as Marcele and the Maxime Girls in the U.S. version

With Una Merkel and George Barbier

Minna Gombell as Marcele in the French-language film with Chevalier and the Maxime Girls

in luster. Let that be spiked at once. He has never been better in voice nor charm.

And *Weekly Variety* reported:

In the leads, Lubitsch picked a double plum out of the talent grab bag. Maurice Chevalier and Jeanette MacDonald both are aces as Danilo and Sonia. The former Paramount pair once again works beautifully in harness, with this one a cinch to enhance Miss MacDonald's already high rating as a singer and looker, and a good bet to regain much of the ground lost by Chevalier in the last couple of years.

In the *New Republic,* Otis Ferguson said:

Chevalier's gifts are not too rangy, but he can balance more ladies on the point of a French accent than might be thought possible, and Ernst Lubitsch has handled him here to best advantage.

In the *Los Angeles Examiner,* one of the ladies enchanted by Chevalier, Louella Parsons, said:

Maurice Chevalier, the captivating Frenchman, who has too long been put into roles that have given him no chance to be the debonair character that Paris loves, is a charming Prince Danilo. He chants his songs and does his wooing in a way guaranteed to make the women of the world dissatisfied with their own romances.

Edwin Schallert, in the *Los Angeles Times,* said:

The Lubitsch picture is done lightly throughout. It is a pleasant revival. It lacks the ironic tinge Erich von Stroheim's silent version possessed when it was new. There is charm and effervescence instead permeating, and entertainment. One possibly should not ask for more.

A 20TH CENTURY PICTURE 1935

With Ann Sothern, doing "Rhythm in the Rain"

Executive Producer, Darryl F. Zanuck. Associate Producers, William Goetz and Raymond Griffith. Directed by Roy Del Ruth. Screenplay by Bess Meredyth and Hal Long. Based on the Play, "The Red Cat," by Rudolph Lothar and Hans Adler. Photographed by Barney McGill and Peverell Marley. Music Arranged and Conducted by Alfred Newman. Choreography by Dave Gould. Chief Sound Engineer, E. H. Hansen. Art Direction Supervision by William Darling. Costumes by Albert M. Levy. Merle Oberon's Gowns by Omar Kiam. Edited by Allen McNeill and Sherman Todd. Filmed in Hollywood at the Goldwyn Studios and released through United Artists. 83 minutes.

SONGS:

"Singing a Happy Song," "I Was Lucky," "Au Revoir l'Amour" and "Rhythm in the Rain," by Jack Meskill and Jack Stern; "You Took the Words Right Out of My Mouth" by Harold Adamson and Burton Lane; "I Don't Stand a Ghost of a Chance with You" by Victor Young, Ned Washington and Bing Crosby; "Valentine" by André Christien and Albert Willemetz, English Lyrics by Herbert Reynolds (M. E. Rourke); sung by Maurice Chevalier. ("Singing a Happy Song" and "Rhythm in the Rain" also sung by Ann Sothern.)

CAST:

Eugene Charlier and *Fernand, the Baron Cassini,* MAURICE CHEVALIER; *Baroness Genevieve Cassini,* MERLE OBERON; *Mimi,* ANN SOTHERN; *René,* Walter BYRON; *Gustave,* Lumsden Hare; *Henri,* Robert Grieg; *François,* Eric Blore; *Paulet,* Halliwell Hobbes; *Victor,* Philip Dare; *Joseph,* Frank McGlynn, Sr.; *Morizet,* Ferdinand Munier; *Perishot,* Ferdinand Gottschalk; *Josephine,* Barbara Leonard; *Premier,* Georges Renavent; *Stage Manager,* Olin Howland; *Bit Rubber,* Sailor Vincent; *Doorman,* Robert Graves; *Second Doorman,* Paul Kruger; *Usherettes:* Olga Borget, Irene Bentley, Vivian Martin, Jenny Gray, Doris Morton; *Butler,* Joseph E. Bernard; *Male Secretary,* Albert Pollet; *Airport Official,* Perry Ivins; *Doctor,* Mario Dominici; *Page Boy,* Paul Toien; *Attendants,* Lew Hicks, Leon Baron; *Ticket Man,* Nam Dibot; *Cafe Waiter,* Harry Holman; *Assistant Stage Manager,* Leonard Walker; *Waiters in Box,* Albert Pollet, Max Barwyn; *Bearded Men:* Ed Reinach, Joe Mack, Pop Garson, Bruce Covington, Charles Hagen, Adolph Faylaver, Harry Milton, Conrad Seidermann, Austin Browne; *Girls in Bar:* Marbeth Wright, Lucille Lund, Jeanne Hart, Joan Woodbury, Bernadene Hayes, Marie Wells, Fay Worth, Maryan Dowling; *Girl Models:* Pauline Rosebrook, Shirley Hughes, Dixie McKinley, Libby Marks, Rosa Milano, Zandra Dvorak; *Bartenders:* Roy Seagus, Eugene Beday, Harry Semek, Hans Schum, Alex Chevron, Luis Hanore, René Mimieux, Dick Allen, Henri Runique; *Waiters:* Bob Von Dobeneck, Al Mazzola, Bill O'Brien, Al Constance, Jack Raymond, Boris Fedotoff; *Girls in Shell:* Audrey Hall, Pokey Champion, Rita Dunn, Claudia Fargo, Myra Jones, Billie Lee, Mary Jane Hodge; *Girls in Secretary Number:* Helen Mann, Joan Sheldon, Jill Evans, Barbara Roberts, Angela Blue, Nell Rhoades, June Gale, Mae Madison; *Girls in Hat Store:* Jenny Gray, Thaya Foster, Ruth Day, Barbara Beall, Gail Goodson, Virginia Dabney; *Principals in Montage:* Wedgwood Nowell, Barlowe Borland, Anders Van Haden, John Ince, Wilson Millar, Yorke Sherwood, Cyril Thornton, Vesey O'Davoran, Robert Cody.

With Merle Oberon

With leading ladies Merle Oberon (U.S. version), and Natalie Paley (French version)

From the French-language version with Natalie Paley

With Merle Oberon and Walter Byron in the U.S. version

Filming the English-language version with Merle Oberon and Roy Del Ruth

As "Charlier," doing his imitation of "Baron Cassini"

STORY:

Because a financial crisis has put his fortune in jeopardy, Baron Cassini is confronted with a situation that makes it necessary for him to be in two places at the same time. Electing to attend a secret business meeting at the same time his presence at a ball is mandatory, the Baron leaves his business partners in a desperate situation. Their hasty solution is to hire Eugene Charlier, a Folies Bergère comic famous for his uncanny imitation of the Baron, to impersonate the Baron at the ball. And since the deception is only to be enforced for a few hours, the Baroness, lately estranged from her husband, is not told about it.

Romantically attracted to the Baroness, who is seemingly repelling her husband's attentions, Charlier learns that the Baron has been seeing a great deal of Mimi, his stage partner. The following day, when the Baron does not return, Charlier is again recruited to impersonate him. While in his disguise, he convinces Mimi that her affair with the Baron cannot continue. Disheartened at first, Mimi later realizes her heart really belongs to Charlier.

Ultimately, the Baron, who has brought off a brilliant financial coup which restores his fortune, returns. Intrigued by his wife's romantic attitude, he learns that Charlier has severed *his* romance with Mimi, and the Baroness knows all about it. The Baron, aware that his foolish indiscretions almost jeopardized his marriage to the woman he really loves, is now confronted with a gnawing speculation about how far Charlier went to restore his wife's love and whether or not she had any inkling of the impersonation.

L'HOMME DES FOLIES BERGÈRE

Released by United Artists, this 20th Century Picture was a simultaneously filmed French-language version of *Folies Bergère,* directed by Roy Del Ruth. The French-language dialog was written by Marcel Achard and the song lyrics by Albert Willemetz. Maurice Chevalier repeated his dual roles, but Natalie Paley played *Baroness Cassini* and Sim Viva played *Mimi.* Others in the cast included: André Berley, Jacques Louvigny, Fernand Ledoux, H. Ramsey Hill, André Cheron, Jules Raucourt, Ferdinand Munier, Marcelle Corday, Barbara Leonard, Georges Renavent, Albert Pollet, Mario Dominici and Olga Borget. 83 minutes.

COMMENTS AND CRITIQUES:

Soon after producing *42nd Street* (1933), Darryl F. Zanuck became enmeshed in his well-known labor union dispute at Warner Bros. and resigned. He was immediately hired as executive producer of 20th-Century Pictures, in charge of all productions. One of his ambitions at the newly formed company was to create a spectacular musical more lavish than *42nd Street.* Consequently, after a lion hunting safari in Africa in 1934, he stopped over in Paris before returning to Hollywood just long enough to acquire the world-wide rights to use the name of the Folies Bergère as a film title.

Two U.S. bistro operators immediately filed suits to prevent this because their similarly named nightclubs would be exploited without recompense to the owners. Each suit, however, automatically cancelled the other and no court would uphold their claims.

Charles Boyer declined the lead and suggested to Zanuck that he get his good friend Maurice Chevalier to do it. Having completed *The Merry Widow* and having no immediate plans for him, MGM agreed and Chevalier was delighted.

The musical numbers were lavishly staged and generous enough to enhance the double identity–*double entendre* plot which, it turned out, was versatile enough to be remade twice: as *That Night in Rio* in 1941, and *On the Riviera* in 1952.

The French-language version included musical sequences in which the chorus girls performed as the actual showgirls did at the world famous showplace—bare-chested. But when this version played at U.S. art houses, these numbers were replaced with those in the English-language version.

Both versions were happily received. In *The New York Times,* André Sennwald said:

M. Chevalier is excellent in his double role and he succeeds in varying his manner sufficiently so that the frantic confusions of the farce are reasonably intelligible, if not startlingly novel. In fact, the straightforward narrative phases of the picture are played with such charm by M. Chevalier, Miss Merle Oberon, and Miss Ann Sothern that they are rather fun.

With Ann Sothern and chorus

And in the *Los Angeles Examiner,* Louella Parsons said:

Folies Bergère is a natural so far as that attractive debonair Frenchman, Maurice Chevalier, is concerned. He fairly radiates that expressive personality of his, singing, dancing, making love and proving himself so magnetic the ladies should flock in large numbers to where it is being shown.

Weekly Variety, reviewing the French language version said:

This is one of the two or three good French language films made in Hollywood during the past four years and is a creditable job . . . Rumor had it that the French version had been made a good deal more risqué than the original. If so, it doesn't show as screened here (New York City, April 1936).

NOTE:

Fox records credit Roy Del Ruth with the direction of the French-language version but Chevalier and Robert Florey both contend that Marcel Achard was the director.

A LES FILMS MARQUIS PRODUCTION 1936

With Josette Day

With Josette Day

Produced and Directed by Julien Duvivier. Screenplay by Charles Vidiac, Charles Spaak and Maurice Chevalier. Music and Lyrics by Borel-Clerc, Michel Emer and Vincent Scotto. Filmed in France in 1936 and released in the U.S. by Trio Films, Inc. on November 20, 1940, where it opened at the 55th Street Playhouse in New York City. 93 minutes.

CAST:

Alfred Boulard, MAURICE CHEVALIER; *Mona Talia,* ELVIRE POPESCO; *Suzanne Petit,* JOSETTE DAY; *Cormier de la Creuse,* AL ERME; *Mother Boulard,* Marcelle Geniat; *Milo,* Robert Lynen; *Suzanne's Sister,* Paulette Elambert; *The Grand Old Lady,* Marguerite Deval; *The Poet,* Pizani; *The Painter,* Fernand Fabre; *The Flower Girl,* Renée Devillers; *An Old Actor,* Aimos.

STORY:

Alfred Boulard, an electrician aspiring to be a music hall singer, witnesses a street accident in which Mona Talia, a great French tragedienne, is critically injured. He volunteers as a blood donor and is credited with saving the actress's life.

Proclaimed the man of the hour by newspapers, Albert finds himself the center of admiration, worshipped by a public who had not previously given him a second glance. He is given 10,000 francs for the publishing rights to his life story and when Mona Talia recovers, she invites him to be a guest at her chateau. But Suzanne, his sweetheart, implores him not to accept by telling him he will be out of his element. Her plea falls on deaf ears.

But after an elegant *soirée,* at which he realizes the guests are mere sycophants and the hostess is a blatant mantrap, Alfred returns to Paris and tells Suzanne she was right. Recovering from his momentary delusions of grandeur, he's not too surprised to learn there is a new "man of the hour" being worshipped for having aided Maurice Chevalier!

COMMENTS AND CRITIQUES:

It took four years for *L'Homme du Jour* to cross the Atlantic and be exhibited, briefly, on U.S. screens.

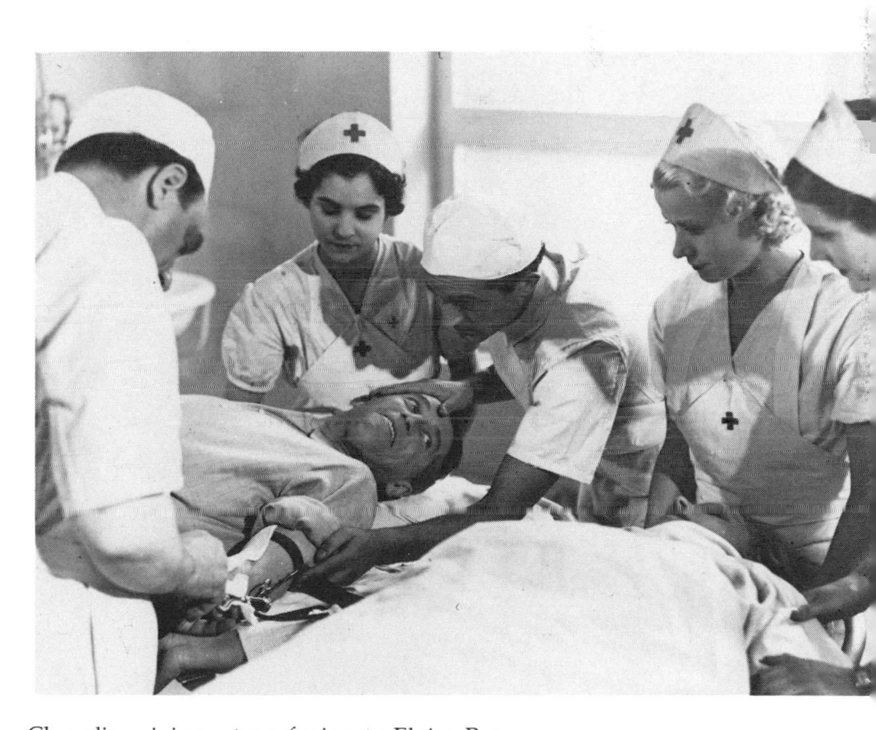

Chevalier giving a transfusion to Elvire Popesco

Chevalier's departure from Hollywood after completing *Folies Bergère* had columnists speculating whether or not he would ever return while voicing their dismay over his pre-war European films which, without exception, were all considered inferior to his U.S. films.

In *The New York Times,* Theodore Strauss said:

Now that the spate of French films is coming rapidly to a close, the Fifty-fifth Street Playhouse hurries forward with another last-minute offering entitled *The Man of the Hour.* It would be pleasant to greet it with more than ordinary ceremony for it brings back the infectiously chucklesome presence of Maurice Chevalier, a little older now, but still sparkling. It has been directed by Julien Duvivier, well known in these parts as one of France's defter directors, and it has occasionally the slyly sophisticated touch that is the hallmark of French comedy. But the truth is that the film does not improve on an obvious idea. Its gayety is thin and it never dances along as a comedy should.

And *Sight and Sound* said:

Whether through an excessive desire to display the talents of his star, Maurice Chevalier, or whatever reason, Julien Duvivier has not made an especially satisfying film. Chevalier plays an electrician with stage-hankerings, who gives his blood to save a famous tragedienne, so earning momentary notoriety—a notoriety which departs as quickly as it came, when he disappoints the tragedienne's passionate designs on him. The idea's satirical possibilities are expanded on in the earlier sequences; but the climax comes prematurely and weakly halfway through, and after this the film just meanders. Chevalier is his usual cheerful self, and for that matter the external technique of direction, the handling of crowds, of camera-movements, and so forth, shows a practised hand. But the film has neither unity of structure nor continuity of mood; and since Duvivier has had a personal finger in the script; he can hardly claim to have been let down by his material.

AVEC LE SOURIRE
(WITH A SMILE)
A PATHÉ PICTURE 1936

With André Lefaur and Marie Glory

With Marie Glory

Produced and Directed by Maurice Tourneur. Screenplay by Louis Verneuill, based on his play, "Avec le Sourire." Photographed by Thiraud and Nee. Music and Lyrics by Marcel Lattes and Borrel Clerc. Art Direction and Set Designs by Carre and Cartigny. Released by Malmar Distributors in the U.S. and first shown on February 4, 1939, at the 55th Street Playhouse, New York City. The French language version released in Europe ran 90 minutes. The version shown in the U.S., with English titles by Herman G. Weinberg, ran 80 minutes.

CAST:

Victor Larnois, MAURICE CHEVALIER; *Gisele,* MARIE GLORY; *M. Villary,* André Lefaur; *Mme. Villary,* Paule Andral; *Pascaud,* Marcel Vallee; *Opera Superintendant,* Marcel Simon; *Cashier,* Milly Mathis.

STORY:

Arriving in Paris penniless, Victor Larnois, a charming and polished confidence man, meets an ambitious chorus girl, Gisele, who works at the Palace Music Hall where he surreptitiously gets the doorman discharged so he can take over his job. Once married to Gisele, Victor is promoted to a position as secretary for the theatre proprietors. By manipulating the accounts, he manages a falling out between partners. Unaware of his plotting, the surviving partner, M. Villary, makes Victor co-owner. But with the help of Gisele, he is soon able to swindle Villary into selling out his share at a loss.

Financially affluent, Victor's aspirations for social recognition are satisfied when, after a blackmail plot, he becomes impresario of the Paris Opera House. At the crest of his triumph, Victor encounters his destitute ex-partner, Villary, whom he hires as his secretary in a moment of rare *noblesse oblige.* Smugly content with his gesture, Victor fails to realize that Villary is now in the same position he was when he began his iniquitous climb to the top.

COMMENTS AND CRITIQUES:

Because of censorship, and a dearth of fully explanatory sub-titles, the version of *Avec le Sourire* exhibited in the U.S. lacked the marvelously ironic black humor of the version released in Europe. There the climax is the one recounted above but in the U.S. version the climax has *Victor* explaining to *Villary* that *savoir faire,* and a disarming smile, are all one needs to achieve business success. All of which is meant to imply that Victor is now an acceptable hero instead of a contented con artist who has become so pompous he's unaware that he has put the enginery of his downfall into the hands of one of his victims.

Weekly Variety said:

Chevalier's role is well tailored and gives him a characterization into which he can dig his teeth . . . English titling hardly does justice to French dialog and there are several long passages without any suitable translation. May be due to parts of the script being censorable. One title, however, is a gem. Situation has anonymous letter arousing a woman's jealousy over husband's reported indiscretions. Ringing for her maid, madame commands, "Fetch my hat, my coat, a revolver and a taxi!"

In the *Motion Picture Herald,* George Spires said:

Sparkling entertainment, with ample opportunity for Chevalier to use the mimicry that made him so well liked in this country.

As the doorman, the first step in his climb to become impresario of the Paris Opera House

Getting the doorman fired so he can take over the job

THE BELOVED VAGABOND

ASSOCIATED BRITISH FILM DISTRIBUTORS 1936

With Betty Stockfeld

Produced by Ludovico Toeplitz. Directed by Kurt (Curtis) Bernhardt. Screenplay by Hugh Mills, Walter Creighton and Arthur Wimperis, based on the novel, "The Beloved Vagabond," by William J. Locke. Photographed by Franz Planer. Music and Lyrics by Milhaud, Mireille and Heymann. Musical Direction by Leslie Bridgewater. Edited by Doug Meyers. Produced in England, 78 minutes. Version distributed in the U.S. by Columbia Pictures, 68 minutes.

SONGS:

"The Reason Is You" and a selection of traditional French melodies and folk songs, sung by Maurice Chevalier.

CAST:

Paragot, MAURICE CHEVALIER; *Joanna,* BETTY STOCKFELD; *Blanquette,* MARGARET LOCKWOOD; *Asticot,* Desmond TESTER; *Comte de Verneuil,* Austin Trevor; *Major Walters,* Peter Haddon; *Mr. Rushworth,* Charles Carson; *Madame Boin,* Cathleen Nesbitt; *Concièrge,* Barbara Gott; *Café Proprietress,* Amy Veness.

STORY:

In love with his employer's daughter, Joanna, and disillusioned when she decides to resolve her father's financial dilemma by marrying a wealthy suitor, André Paragot gives up his job as an architect and returns to France.

Embarking on an idyllic summer to forget his broken heart, Paragot, accompanied by his young charge, Asticot, come upon Blanquette, a gypsy girl who supports herself wandering the countryside playing the accordion. Eventually, Asticot, who plays a drum, and Paragot, who sings, find themselves drawn into a minstrel trio with Blanquette. Weeks later, while stopping at a countryside inn, Paragot realizes Blanquette is in love with him. In order to spare her feelings and not allow her to become more emotionally involved, he says he must take Asticot back to England so the boy can return to school.

Back in London, Paragot encounters Joanna again, discovering she did not marry after all. Delighted at first, it doesn't take him too long to realize Joanna is a material-minded woman who could never be happy with a simple life. Deciding he doesn't love her after all, Paragot returns to Normandy to search out Blanquette and tell her.

With Margaret Lockwood

With Margaret Lockwood and Desmond Tester

LE VAGABOND BIEN-AIMÉ

A simultaneously filmed French-language version of *The Beloved Vagabond,* directed by Kurt Bernhardt, with Maurice Chevalier, Betty Stockfeld, Austin Trevor and Charles Carson repeating their roles. Others in the cast: Helen Robert, Serge Grave, Madeleine Guitty, Mad Siame and Fernand Ledoux. 80 minutes.

COMMENTS AND CRITIQUES:

First filmed in 1916 by Pathé, and remade by Carlyle Blackwell, with himself as star, in 1924, *The Beloved Vagabond* was acquired by Ludovico Toeplitz around the time he was making an international name for himself as co-producer of *The Private Life of Henry VIII.* Originally planned as a Russ Columbo film, the accidental death of the singing star caused Toeplitz to negotiate a deal with Paramount to use Cary Grant, then in England doing another film. When Grant rejected the script, it was offered to Hollywood expatriate Maurice Chevalier, who accepted with alacrity when he realized much of it would be filmed in France.

Whatever elusive ingredient it was in the script which attracted Toeplitz as producer, Bernhardt as director and Chevalier as star, failed to materialize in the completed film(s).

After the London premiere, *Weekly Variety* said:

Absent from American screens for about three years now, Maurice Chevalier returns in an English-made which gets release on this side by Columbia. It will not hasten his return to Hollywood, in case the French singing star is interested, and in all probability will not encourage further American release of anything he does on the other side. The Toeplitz production with Chevalier and an all-English cast, teasingly entitled *The Beloved Vagabond,* is rather shoddy entertainment and will have difficulty grabbing more than passing notice on double bills . . . Chevalier does okay with the weak material handed him. He is deserving of much better.

In the *New York World-Telegram,* William Boehnel said:

Since this department has pleasant memories of earlier Chevalier films, nothing would please it more than to write cheerfully of *The Beloved Vagabond.* But the bitter truth compels me to report not only has M. Chevalier been unhappy in the script he has chosen for his return to the cinema, but also that M. Chevalier is only a shadow of his former self.

NOTE:

Lest confusion reign among readers over some of the comments in these reviews, it should be remembered that this filmography is chronological in the order the films were produced. Hence, two European films made previous to *The Beloved Vagabond, L'Homme du Jour* and *Avec le Sourire,* were not imported for U.S. showings until much later.

A TRIO PICTURE 1938

With June Knight

Being restrained by bailiffs upon learning he has been found guilty of murder.

With Jack Buchanan

A Jack Buchanan Production. Produced and Directed by René Clair. Screenplay by Geoffrey Kerr. Adapted by Carlo Rima, from the novel, "La Mort En Fuite," by Lois le Guriadec. Photographed by Phil Tannura. Orchestrations and Musical Direction by Van Phillips. Released in Great Britain by General Film Distributors, 78 minutes. Distributed in the U.S., in 1941, by Monogram Pictures: 72 minutes. Filmed in England.

SONGS:

"It All Belongs to You," music and lyrics by Cole Porter, sung by Maurice Chevalier. "We're Two Old Buddies," by Van Phillips and Jack Buchanan, sung by Chevalier and Buchanan.

CAST:

Francois Verrier, MAURICE CHEVALIER; *Teddy Enton,* JACK BUCHANAN; *Grace Gatwick,* JUNE KNIGHT, *Sonia,* Marta Labarr; *Helena,* Gertrude Musgrove; *Interpreter,* Charles Lefeaux; *Producer,* Gary Marsh; *Assistant Stage Manager,* Wallace Douglas; *Sir George Bickory,* Felix Aylmer; *Sir Edward Phring,* C. Denier Warren; *Judge,* D. J. Williams; *Taxi Driver,* Robb Wilton; *Night Porter,* Gibb McLaughlin; *Dresser,* Elliot Mason; *Prison Governor,* Athole Stewart; *Neighbour,* J. Abercomie; *Englishman,* Guy Middleton; *President of Tribunal,* George Hayes; *Passport Official,* W. Fazan; *Property Man,* Mark Daly; *Firing Squad Officer,* George Benson; *Press Agent,* Joss Ambler; *Solicitor,* H. R. Hignett; *Prison Guards,* Wally Patch, Hall Gordon.

With Jack Buchanan

With Wallace Douglas and Jack Buchanan

STORY:

During the dress rehearsal of a tacky musical revue, song and dance men François Verrier and Teddy Enton find their routine has been dropped from the show on orders from the publicity mad star, Grace Gatwick. Convinced professional jealousy motivated her, the two entertainers devise a plot to get into the limelight and back in front of the footlights.

The plan is for Enton to disappear and hide in one of the Balkan states and for Verrier to confess he's murdered him. Then, when Verrier is about to be convicted of homicide, Enton will dramatically reappear and save him. All goes as planned until a revolution detains Enton from returning in time for the trial and Verrier, the self-confessed "killer," is convicted and sentenced to be executed.

Back in the Balkan state Enton is mistaken for an enemy general and marched off to face a firing squad. By a ruse, he effects his escape and returns to London hoping to prevent a grave miscarriage of justice. At the last minute, however, circumstances force him to recruit the help of Grace Gatwick who, after Verrier is exonerated, is back in the headlines being proclaimed a national heroine.

COMMENTS AND CRITIQUES:

René Clair's *Break the News,* an English-language re-make of André Berthomieu's *Le Mort en Fuite,* was anticipated for over three years by discerning U.S. film enthusiasts familiar with the director's earlier classics and perplexed about the long delay between completion (late 1936) and importation (early 1941).

After its first trade showing in Britain, the *Motion Picture Herald* said:

Both the stars of this lively British comedy have international repute, and René Clair, highly graded French director, whose *Ghost Goes West* will be remembered, has given *Break the News* a certain Gallic flavor, and inset physical slapstick with wit and whimsy which should register with the more discerning audience. Besides, there are polished technical qualities, inspired casting in the minor characters, and, above all, a most ingenious script.

On January 2, 1941, some three years after the

above review came out, in *The New York Times,* Bosley Crowther said:

Should old acquaintance be forgot, perhaps we should remind that the René Clair who produced and directed the British-made *Break the News,* which inaugurated the new year yesterday at the Bryant, is the same René Clair who directed *The Ghost Goes West, Le Million, A Nous la Liberté,* and other distinguished films. Certainly you'd barely guess it from *Break the News* itself. For the only generic resemblance which this moderately amusing comedy with music bears to previous Clair films lies in the sauciness of its original idea and in the hectic confusion which accumulates toward the end. Along the way there is little to suggest the old Clair wit and humor.

In *The Nation,* James Agee reported:

Break the News was made in England by René Clair, with Jack Buchanan and Maurice Chevalier. It isn't at all on the level with those Clair films of which the mere recall can bring me tears of admiration and of a detached sort of pride; but it is full of ease and fun and extravagant but unstrained irony, enjoyable of themselves, and worth watching too because they so clearly indicate that, though England was not a good place for Clair to work, it was not, like this country, a hell on earth.

In the *Los Angeles Times,* Philip K. Scheuer, said:

While one rejoices at glimpsing Chevalier once more, his performance and his role never really get together. . . . The piece has its moments but a more apt title, on the whole, might have been *Break the News Gently.*

With Jack Buchanan

PIEGES
(PERSONAL COLUMN)

A SPEVA FILM 1939

Produced by Michel Safra. Directed by Robert Siodmak. Screenplay by Jacques Companeez and Ernest Neuville. Dialog by Simon Gantillon. Photographed by R. Voinquel. Music by Michel Michelet. Art Direction and Set Decoration by Wakevich and Colasson. Edited by Yvonne Martin. Filmed at the Pathé-Joinville Studios in France, 100 minutes. Distributed in the U.S. by Pax Films (89 minutes).

SONGS:

"Elle Pleurait Comme Une, Madeleine," music by R. Reville, lyrics by Maurice Vander, and "Mon Amour," music by Fredo Gardoni and Jean Chavoit, lyrics by Willemetz; both sung by Maurice Chevalier.

CAST:

Robert Fleury, MAURICE CHEVALIER; *Pears,* ERICH Von STROHEIM; *Bremontiere,* Pierre RENOIR; *Adrienne,* Marie DEA; *Tenier,* André Brunot; *Batol,* Temerson; *Maxime,* Jacques Varennes; *Valerie,* Madeleine Geoffroy; *Police Inspectors:* Rognoni, André Nicolle; *Housekeeper,* Julienne Paroli; *Oglou,* Henri Bry; *Cook,* Mady Berry; *Patrons:* Henri Cremieux, André Roanne.

STORY:

When questioned by the police in connection with the disappearance of her beautiful young roommate, Adrienne, a taxi dancer, gives them an account of the missing girl's last known movements which coincide exactly with circumstances involving other missing, and presumed murdered, girls. Believing all the missing girls met their doom after answering an advertisement in the personal column of a Paris newspaper, the police hire Adrienne to work as an undercover agent and answer all advertisements which offer employment to young, single girls. With the knowledge that she has the security of police surveillance, Adrienne goes about making arrangements to meet a bizarre assortment of men who all, for one reason or another, have placed an ad in the personal column offering employment to a young, single girl.

Among the suspects she encounters are a couturier, a hotel manager and Robert Fleury, a nightclub entertainer ostensibly looking to hire a new maid, with whom Adrienne falls in love. Each advertiser is investigated and cleared of suspicion and the cases remain unsolved.

Then, just before Adrienne is about to marry Fleury, he is arrested and charged with having murdered the missing girls. At his trial, piece after piece of damning evidence is introduced and although he steadfastly maintains his innocence, Fleury is convicted and condemned to die. But believing with all her heart that he is innocent, Adrienne sets a trap for the real killer with herself as bait.

COMMENTS AND CRITIQUES:

Pièges was Maurice Chevalier's last pre-WW II film and also one of the very last films made in free

With Marie Dea

With Marie Dea

With André Brunot

With Marie Dea and Pierre Renoir

France. A print of it was smuggled out of the country after the occupation and shipped to the U.S. in a convoy stalked by German submarines. And although it escaped the Nazi torpedoes, it did not escape the U.S. censor's scissors. Consequently, all scenes alluding to the sexual aberrations of some of the murder suspects were excised.

The 1947 remake, produced in Hollywood by Hunt Stromberg, was called *Lured* and starred Lucille Ball and George Sanders in the leads with Boris Karloff cast as the red herring, assuming the roles originally played by Marie Dea, Chevalier and Erich von Stroheim. The U.S. version also retained one of the songs, "Mon Amour," which was sung in a nightclub sequence by an unbilled songstress.

Released in the U.S. in early 1941 with English subtitles and called *Personal Column,* it was well received by the critics. In *The New York Times,* Theodore Strauss said:

Even after running the gauntlet of the censorial shears, *Personal Column,* the new French film at the Little Carnegie, remains a beguiling, if occasionally frustrated, entertainment. That it has flaws in construction, however, is due not so much to the censors as to the author and director, who begin in the piquantly picaresque fashion of *Carnet de Bal* but toward the end plunge abruptly into psychological melodrama. The fault is basic, but it cannot detract from the fact that the separate sequences are written with quixotic wit, that their Gallic frankness has been only partly hushed and that Maurice Chevalier is still the best definition of what Frenchmen mean by *joie de vivre.*

In the *Los Angeles Times,* John L. Scott said:

There is an unusual quality to *Personal Column* and had it been made in this country by the same actors and the same director, Robert Siodmak, it would undoubtably prove something of a sensation. The French dialogue is fairly spicy at times but you would never know it from the English subtitles.

In the *Los Angeles Examiner,* Rosalind Shaffer said:

Personal Column is important for two reasons. It supplies a vehicle for Maurice Chevalier, and offers a very tricky mystery story as well. As for Chevalier, he still puts a song over with the same old personality. As for the story, it is one that keeps developing new twists as it goes along. Refreshingly free of the Hollywood formula, it provides a well-elaborated murder and disappearance mystery in the best French manner.

LE SILENCE EST D'OR
(MAN ABOUT TOWN)

A PATHÉ CINEMA–RKO RADIO PRODUCTION 1945

Chevalier as a silent film director

With Francois Perier

Produced, Directed and Written by René Clair. Assistant Director, Pierre Blondy. Director of Photography, Armand Thirard. Cameraman, Alain Douarinou. Musical Director, George Van Parys. Sound Engineer, Antoine Archimbaud. Art Director, Leon Barsacq. Costumes by Christian Dior. Production Manager, Edouard Lepage. A Societé Nouvelle Pathé Cinema Production, filmed in France. 106 minutes. The 89-minute version released in the U.S. in 1947 had a special prologue and narration, spoken in English by Maurice Chevalier; which was filmed and recorded at the RKO studio in Hollywood under the supervision of associate producer Robert Pirosh.

SONGS:

In the specially filmed prologue of the 89-minute version, Maurice Chevalier sings "Place Pigalle."

CAST:

Emile, MAURICE CHEVALIER; *Jacques,* François Perier; *Madeleine,* Marcelle Derrien; *Lucette,* Dany Robin; *Duperrier,* Robert Pizani; *Curly,* Raymond Cordy; *Cashier,* Paul Olivier; *Celestin,* Roland Armontel.

STORY:

When Madeleine, an innocent young maiden, comes to Paris in the spring of 1906 and is unable to find her father, an itinerant actor, she turns for help to Emile, a middle-aged film director who had been an old flame of her mother's. Learning that her father is on tour, Madeleine accepts Emile's proposal that she spend her time awaiting his return by acting in a film he is making. When she accepts, Emile issues strict orders to his crew that the innocent girl is to be left alone.

Puzzled because the men at the studio do not pursue her, Madeleine tearfully tells Emile that nobody loves her. While comforting her, Emile realizes he loves her and is reluctant to say so. Soon afterward, a young actor named Jacques meets Madeleine on a bus and not knowing she is Emile's protegée, seeks his help in wooing her.

Besides offering Jacques advice on how to woo his mysterious sweetheart, Emile is confronted with the dilemma of giving his film a proper ending and how he can best tell Madeleine how he feels about her. But when he inadvertently learns Madeleine is in love with Jacques, Emile ends his film with the hero, not the villain, winning the heroine. And he gallantly steps aside so Jacques can win Madeleine.

COMMENTS AND CRITIQUES:

Le Silence Est d'Or won first prize at the 1947 Brussels Film Festival and the Critics' Circle Award at the Locarno Festival although it was certainly not vintage René Clair. But it was one of the first postwar French films to get international bookings and both awards seemed to be gestures of encouragement to the French film industry rather than acknowledgements of an exceptional achievement.

But even lacking his usual flair for *Clairbuoyance, Le Silence Est d'Or* and *Man About Town,* the version released in the U.S., were well worth everyone's attention.

In the November 10, 1947 issue of *Life* magazine, *Man About Town* was named Movie of the Week. Said *Life:*

Man About Town is made like a Mack Sennett farce: the two lovers play it straight and everybody else is a comedian. Some scenes are just inventive slapstick, but as a whole *Man About Town* is performed so deftly and with such gaiety that it makes most U.S. comedies seem cruder than Mortimer Snerd. To solve the problem of translation, which hurts most French films at the box office, RKO has an ingenious solution: no subtitles; instead, Chevalier's voice occasionally interrupts the sound track to explain in English what is going on.

In the *New Statesman and Nation,* William Whitebait said:

With *Le Silence Est d'Or* René Clair returns to two early loves: Paris and the silent film. What a pleasure it is—after how many years of exile—to eye the girls on the boulevard, to travel on top of a horse bus, to squeeze and be squeezed in the *promenoir* of a music hall, to wave away the fiddler outside a *café,* only to be told he has been paid by a drunk gentleman to go on repeating the same tune for the rest of the evening! Here again are the cobbles, if not the roofs, of Paris; yes, a familiar ring of people clusters around a street singer. This is a sentimental, a middle-aged occasion, and M. Clair, perhaps wisely, has played safe while (one hopes) getting his hand in. . . . The middle-aged director, by the way, is Maurice Chevalier; he takes a fatherly but brisk interest in girls, and avoids his reflection in the mirror. He doesn't sing or tilt a straw; just acts, with some assurance and charm.

And the *Hollywood Reporter* said:

Two such irrepressible talents as those of Maurice Chevalier and René Clair would have a difficult time in creating anything but the most charming motion picture adventure. This, precisely, is what they have done in *Man About Town*—a frothy and beguiling little comedy which moves along at a completely abandoned pace, thanks to a story singularly free of plot complexities. As smooth as a fine liqueur and as bubbly as good champagne, it has the warmth of the first and the giddy kick of the latter.

With Francois Perier

With Marcelle Derrien and Francois Perier

A DISCINA INTERNATIONAL PICTURE 1949

With Annie Ducaux

Produced by Michel Safra and André Paulve. Written and Directed by Marc-Gilbert Sauvajon. Adapted from the play, "Le Roi," by R. de Flers, G. A. Caillavet and E. Arene. Photographed by Robert LeFebvre. Musical Score by Jean Marion. Production Designer, Guy de Gastyne. Sets by André Boutie. Edited by Roger Dwyre. Filmed in France. 100 minutes.

SONGS:

"C'est Fini" and "Danser la Cachucha" sung by Maurice Chevalier.

CAST:

The King, MAURICE CHEVALIER; *Therese Marnix,* Annie Ducaux; *Mme. Beaudrier,* Sophie Desmarets; *Beaudrier,* Alfred Adam; *LeLorrain,* Jean Wall; *Blond,* Robert Murzeau; *Marquis de Chamarande,* Robert Vattier; *Postmaster General,* Felix Paquet; *Minister of Commerce,* Henry Charrett; *Marcel Rivelot,* François Joux; *Count Martin,* Delaitre.

STORY:

After arriving in Paris on a mission of state, the King of Cerdania becomes the center of an international incident when he is hit in the face with a cream puff thrown by the beautiful but impulsive wife of Senator Beaudrier. Ordered to placate the visiting monarch and hush up the threatening scandal, Senator Beaudrier discovers the King is not only interested in the Senator's wife but also in his mistress, Therese Marnix, a beautiful actress, and had once been her lover.

By doing his utmost to keep his wife and mistress away from the King, the Senator inadvertently makes it so easy for the monarch to seduce them, he signs the treaty (which prompted his visit in the first place), awards the Senator a decoration and a cabinet post, and then returns to Cerdania convinced his old charm is as potent as ever.

COMMENTS AND CRITIQUES:

A durable French stage farce (it had also been filmed in France in 1936 with Raimu and Victor Francen), *Le Roi* was not quite so hearty an entry on the U.S. art house circuits when, as *A Royal Affair,* it opened to favorable reviews and poor business in 1950.

The *Los Angeles Times* said:

Monsieur Maurice Chevalier isn't as young as he used to be, but he still has enough charm to lure the gals and others to the Fine Arts and Guild Theatres. Once inside they wouldn't leave on a bet, finding plenty of entertainment in the star's gay current vehicle, *A Royal Affair,* pervaded by subtle Gallic humor. Chevalier's graceful stepping, his provocative French songs, his debonair acting, and his fascinatingly crooked smile make this comedy role fit him like a glove.

With Alfred Adam and Sophie Desmarets

With Sophie Desmarets

The *New York Times* said:

As the dallying King, Maurice Chevalier, while not precisely the dashing troubadour of yore, is a smiling and mature gent, who tries valiantly to put some life into several of the film's undistinguished songs.

And *Weekly Variety* reported:

Maurice Chevalier, "The King" himself, bewigged and youthful looking, gives the pic a nostalgic air. The Chevalier charm is in good evidence, and he gets a chance to deliver a few songs in his usual socko manner, of which the ditty "C'est Fini" looks like a comer. On its frothy theme, good treatment and Chevalier's pull, pic will please in all stateside situations.

The *Independent Film Journal* was even more enthusiastic:

Class audiences and French-speaking patrons will find *A Royal Affair* completely captivating cinema. This mixture of frothy comedy and a Gallic abundance of sex, colored with the unique personality of Maurice Chevalier, brims over with good humor and charm. The plot throws complication upon complication, but the spirited acting and the film's swift pace compensate for this weakness. Chevalier's name has a draw in the foreign film circuit and ticket buyers will be perfectly satisfied with the singer's ability to put across a few pleasant musical numbers.

MA POMME (JUST ME)

A DISCINA INTERNATIONAL PICTURE 1950

With Sophie Desmarets

With Jane Marken and Jean Wall

With Raymond Bussieres

Produced by Michel Safra and André Paulve. Written and Directed by Marc-Gilbert Sauvajon. Photographed by Henri Alekan. Musical Score and Song by Jean Marion. Sets by Jean D'Eaubonne. Edited by Roger Dwyre. Filmed in France. 90 minutes.

SONG:

"Ma Pomme—The Hobo's Serenade," sung by Maurice Chevalier.

CAST:

Ma Pomme, MAURICE CHEVALIER; *M. Peuchat,* Jean Wall; *Mme. Peuchat,* Sophie Desmarets; *Mme. Deply,* Jane Marken; *Claire,* Vera Norman; *Dubuisson,* Jacques Baumer; *Fricotard,* Raymond Bussières; *Valentin,* Felix Paquet; *Jacques Turpin,* Dynam; *Le Patron,* Jean Hebey.

STORY:

Ma Pomme, a happy-go-lucky hobo, rejects the fortune left to him by an unknown ancestor after learning he would have to be executor of the estate, as well as co-heir. But because they cannot inherit their share unless he does accept, the other two co-inheritors, M. Peuchat, a greedy banker, and Mme. Deply, a compulsive gambler who works as a hatcheck attendant, implore him to change his mind.

He does—but not until a fourth heir is discovered: an airline hostess, named Claire, who is in actual need of money in order to marry the impoverished young man she loves. After the will is executed, Claire, unhappy with her marriage, begins an affair with M. Peuchat—and Mme. Deply, who breaks the bank at the Monte Carlo casino, dies in shock. Ma Pomme, loathing the life of the rich, gets ulcers as he watches his co-inheritors disintegrate.

Unable to go on living as a man of wealth, Ma Pomme uses his inheritance to build a rest camp for hobos and he jauntily sets forth once more as a knight of the open road.

COMMENTS AND CRITIQUES:

Although it's possible to watch *Ma Pomme* now and justly proclaim it as a 1950's film which anticipated the hippie-oriented culture of the 1960's, at the time of its release it seemed more like a hollow

echo of too many prewar Hollywood films which were much more adroit at making the Depression seem less oppressive to laugh-hungry audiences.

In *The New York Times*, Bosley Crowther said:

After fifty years of cheerful entertaining—and, believe it nor not, it's been that long that crinkle-faced Maurice Chevalier has been tossing his banter to the world—it is sad to behold this old favorite playing a wistful and aging bum in a drab little bit of French flim-flam that goes by the name of *Ma Pomme*. . . . For a man who has made so many happy and has yet a mellowed talent to expend, there must be something more vigorous, more optimistic than this.

In *Cue* magazine, Jesse Zunser said:

It would be a far more amusing and convincing homily if it had more wit about it. As it is, the author's dull writing and plodding direction deprive it of much of the amusement inherent in his theme, and M. Chevalier's self-conscious playing of the tramp doesn't help much, either. There is some fun, but not as much as we've come to expect in a Chevalier comedy.

And the *Motion Picture Herald* said:

Maurice Chevalier tries his hand at a Charlie Chaplinesque portrayal in a French-language comedy drama with only occasional interludes. The great French star's mature charm still shines through a ragged, dirty hobo's outfit even if the story is long drawn-out and intermittently amusing.

And *Newsweek* told the nation that:

Ma Pomme is a French film dedicated to the 50th theatrical anniversary of its distinguished star, Maurice Chevalier. . . . The film is described as "a philosophical comedy set to music," but its thought content is terribly weighted by unfunny ballast and music very far from the Chevalier standard.

A MELODIE-HERZOG FILM 1953

With Margot Hielscher

Produced by H. J. Ewert. Directed by Eric Ode. Screenplay by Aldo von Pinelli and H. F. Kollner. Photographed by Richard Angst. Music by Heino Gaze. Lyrics by Aldo von Pinelli and Gunther Schwenn. Musical Arrangements by Werner Muller. Sound Recording by Werner Mass. Choreography by Tatjana Gsovsky. Sets by Karl Walter. Edited by Wolfgang Wehrums. Filmed in Germany at the Berlin-Spandau Studios. 100 minutes.

PLAYERS:

Germaine Damar, Walter Giller, Nadja Tiller, Karl Schonbock, Loni Heuser, Walter Cross, Renate Danz, Bully Buhlan, Willi Schaeffers.

INTERNATIONAL GUEST STARS (as themselves):

Margot Hielscher, Johannes Heesters, Lya Assia, Gitta Lind, Rita Paul, Renate Holm, Rudi Schuricke, Friedel Hensch and the Cyprys, The Sunshine Quartet, The Cornel Trio, Tatjana Gsovsky and Her Dancers, Robby Gay, Michael Jary, Peter Kreuder, Friedrich Schroder, Peter Igelhoff, The Rias Dance Orchestra, conducted by Werner Muller, Stan Kenton and His Orchestra and Maurice Chevalier.

STORY:

The daughter of a music teacher (Damar) loves an unsuccessful songwriter (Giller) who has lost faith in his ability. To prove that he really has talent, she sends one of his songs to a publisher and represents it as the work of a famous composer (Schonbock). It becomes an immediate hit but the famous composer denies having written it. Infuriated with his sweetheart, the young composer refuses to admit it's his song until he's appearing on a national broadcast. Then, when he's tricked into thinking the famous composer is after his girl, he accuses him of stealing his song and trying to steal his girl.

COMMENTS AND CRITIQUES:

Advertised as a modern cavalcade of song and Germany's most extravagantly produced musical of the day, *Schlager-Parade* opened in Germany for the 1953 Christmas season and was a tremendous box-office hit. But because none of the "name" musical talents in it, except Maurice Chevalier and Stan Kenton, had any popularity outside of Germany and Paris it was never exported.

In *Die Filmwoche (The Film Weekly)*, Ernst-Michael Quass said:

Let's be polite and admit it, international star Maurice Chevalier, straw hat and all, assisted by Margot Hielscher, sings "Ça-va, Ça-va," and, backed by Stan Kenton and his orchestra, gives the whole thing zest. . . . Walter Riller, who has been so adroit in several recent comedies, isn't very well cast as a down-on-his-luck song composer.

NOTE:

A literate translation of *Schlager-Parade* is, of course, *Hit Parade.* And, curiously enough, although no mention is ever made of it, the plot of this German film, sans the insertion of name guest stars, and with a switch of gender, closely resembles the Republic film *Hit Parade of 1943* which first played in Germany in 1951 when it was called *Change of Heart.* This too may have been one of the factors contributing to its never being exhibited outside of Germany.

Left: Germaine Damar and Walter Giller
Right. Chevalier and chorus girls

CENTO ANNI D'AMORE

A CINES PRODUCTION 1954

Alba Arnova and Jacques Sernas
in the foreground

Produced and Directed by Lionello de Felice. Written by Guido Gozzano, Gabriel D'Annunzio, Giulio Rocca, Marino Moretti, Lionello de Felice and Oreste Biancoli. Photographed by Aldo Tonti. Musical Score by Nino Rota, Mario Nascimbene and Ted Usetti. Art Direction and Set Decoration by Franco Lotti. Edited by Mario Serandrei. Filmed in Italy. 110 minutes.

Cento Anni d'Amore is an anthology film offering a sextet of stories reviewing fashions in love from 1854 to 1954:

GARIBALDINA is about an anti-Garibaldi priest who changes his mind about the new government and urges other citizens to do likewise.

PENDOLIN concerns an unfaithful wife's romance with a hotel porter who only tried to return one of her lost earrings.

PURIFICATION tells of a soldier who is unable to deliver his dying officer's last message to his girl because he thinks she is unworthy.

GOLDEN WEDDING has a couple becoming disillusioned with each other after they celebrate their golden wedding anniversary.

THE LAST TEN MINUTES concerns a condemned man and a priest devising a way in which to spare the widow from knowing the real reason for the execution.

AMORE, 1954 has a divorce-minded young couple reunite after the bride's father makes his son-in-law realize he has misjudged his wife.

CAST:

Maurice Chevalier, Alba Arnova and Jacques Sernas starred in the sixth episode, AMORE, 1954. Players in the other five episodes included Aldo Fabrizi, Irene Galter, Franco Interlenghi, Carol Ninchi, Vittorio De Sica, Nadia Gray, Luigi Cimara, Carlo Campanini, Eduardo de Filippo, Titina de Filippo, Giuletta Masina, Rina Morelli, Ernesto Almirante, Virgilio Riento, Lea Padovani, Gabriele Ferzetti, Xenia Valderi and Laura Gore.

NOTE:

Cento Anni d'Amore was filmed in 1953 and released in Italy, briefly, in 1954. Two years later it had a showing in Paris for a trade audience but it has never been shown, or made available for distribution, in Great Britain or the U.S.

J'AVAIS SEPT FILLES
(MY SEVEN LITTLE SINS)

A KINGSLEY INTERNATIONAL RELEASE 1955

Produced by Francinalp-Faro Films. Directed by Jean Boyer. Screenplay by Serge Veber and Jean Des Vallières. Adapted by Des Vallières and Boyer from a story by Aldo de Benedetti. Photographed in FerraniaColor by Charles Suin. Musical Score and Songs by Fred Freed. Edited by A. Laurent. Filmed in France and Italy. 98 minutes.

SONGS:

"C'est l'Amour" and "Demain J'ai Vingt Ans" sung by Maurice Chevalier.

CAST:

Count André, MAURICE CHEVALIER; *Luisella,* Delia Scala; *Linda,* Colette Ripert; *Lolita,* Maria Frau; *Nadine,* Annick Tanguy; *Pat,* Lucianna Paoluzzi; *Daisy,* Mimi Medard; *Blanchette,* Maria Luisa Da Silva; *Maria,* Gaby Basset; *Antonio,* Paolo Stoppa; *Professor Gorbiggi,* Pasquali; *Edouard,* Louis Velle; *Bertoul,* Robert Destrain.

STORY:

Ensconced in his chateau in southern France, Count André is at work on his amorous memoirs, using a card index he has kept on his love affairs to refresh his memory, when, to his surprise, a beautiful young lady appears, claiming to be his daughter by a long-forgotten love. Delighted, Count André receives her with open arms and extends to her the hospitality of his chateau while he keeps reminding himself to behave toward her like a father.

But the Count suspects he's the victim of a hoax when six other young ladies, equally beautiful, also show up at the chateau and claim to be daughters by other loves of the past. But he keeps his doubts to himself and goes along with the charade until his son, who has been away on a scientific expedition, returns home suddenly and finds seven bogus half-sisters offering him their affection and attention.

When it becomes apparent that his son is romantically attracted to one of the girls, the Count feels it's time to let them all know he knows they are not his daughters. Confirming this, the girls admit the truth: they are members of a stranded theatrical troupe who got ahold of the Count's card-index and decided to pose as his daughters until something turned up on the theatrical horizon.

COMMENTS AND CRITIQUES:

This French-Italian co-production opened in the U.S. in 1956 right after the government lifted its ban on Maurice Chevalier's visa and permitted him to enter the country for a visit, or, if he desired, to work. His rejuvenated popularity and sudden availability resulted in his being invited to appear on the 1957 Academy Award telecast. *J'Avais Sept Filles* was also Chevalier's first appearance before color cameras since making *Paramount on Parade.*

In the *Los Angeles Times,* Edwin Schallert said:

Being as mature as he is now, Chevalier does well to portray a somewhat paternal role, but he is for the most part only a papa *à la mode,* and is still irremediably the dashing blade with the ladies. One never surmises that he is taking his daddyhood seriously, nor does he actually have to in this racy scherzo of a picture. He also sings with style, if not with too much voice, and he is otherwise most engaging in this light portrayal.

In *Cue* magazine, Jesse Zunser said:

Nobody, but nobody in all the world, grows old as gracefully, slowly and waggishly as M. Chevalier. And certainly nobody could carry off this frothy little film fable with the *éclat* and *savoir-faire,* or whatever else you call it, that Maurice can summon at the crack of a smile.

In the *Los Angeles Examiner,* Sara Hamilton said:

The Lip, the Smile, the Straw Hat, the Maurice of Paree, our favorite Frenchman, Chevalier himself, is romping across the Vagabond screen in a delightful bit of fluff titled *My Seven Little Sins. . . .* It's meant to be gay and light and amusing, and it succeeds. Maurice sings as of old, as charming and beguiling as ever.

In the New York *Times,* Bosley Crowther said:

Aging and graying Maurice Chevalier, who plays the leading role, is not, for the most part, unattractive in the embarrassing things he has to do. He manages fairly nicely to make himself tolerable as a French count, with a villa on the Riviera, who is proud of his past as a Don Juan.

With Louis Velle, his seven daughters and Robert Destrain

Chevalier and his seven daughters

With Paolo Stoppa

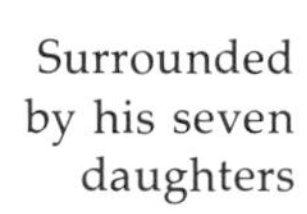

Surrounded by his seven daughters

THE HAPPY ROAD

A KERRY-METRO-GOLDWYN-MAYER RELEASE 1957

Bobby Clark and Brigitte Fossey

Produced and Directed by Gene Kelly. Associate Producer, Noel Howard. Screenplay by Arthur Julian, Joseph Morhaim and Harry Kurnitz. (Based on an original story by Julian and Morhaim.) Photographed by Robert Juillard. Musical Score, Song and Lyrics, by George Van Parys. Art Direction by Alexandre Traunes. Barbara Laage's Clothes by Pierre Balmain. Edited by Borys Lewin. Filmed in France. 100 minutes.

SONG:

"The Happy Road" sung by Maurice Chevalier.

CAST:

Mike Andrews, GENE KELLY; *Suzanne Duval,* BARBARA LAAGE; *General Medworth,* MICHAEL REDGRAVE; *Danny Andrews,* Bobby Clark; *Janine Duval,* Brigitte Fossey; *Docteur Solaise,* Roger Treville; *Helene,* Colette Dereal; *Morgan,* Jess Hahn; *Madame Fallère,* Maryse Martin; *Verbier,* Roger Saget; *Motorcycle Officer,* Van Doude; *Hotel Patron,* Claire Gerard; *Armbruster,* Colin Mann; *Bucheron,* Alexandre Rignault.

Gene Kelly and Barbara Laage

STORY:

Arriving at the Swiss school from which his young son, Danny, has disappeared, Mike Andrews, an American businessman living in Paris, encounters Suzanne Duval, a beautiful divorcee, whose daughter Janine is also missing from school and presumed to be with Danny. Mike, a widower, and Suzanne take an instantaneous dislike to each other although they pool their resources to search for the children when the police haven't located them by nightfall.

Danny's motive for running away from school is to prove to his father that he's self-reliant enough to make it to Paris on his own and therefore capable of living with him there. Janine, smitten with Danny, uses her feminine logic to convince him to take her along to act as interpreter since he cannot speak French. A group of schoolchildren, hearing they are running away from school, help them elude the police and their parents and they later get help from the members of a cross-country bicycle tour. And when they encounter General Medworth, who is handling military maneuvers for a NATO unit, he, too, inadvertently helps them elude their pursuers.

Trailing after them, Mike and Suzanne become involved in cross-country contretemps which, before they arrive in Paris, includes spending a night in jail. Reunited with their children, they discover their animosity toward each other is really more amorous than hostile and that each child could benefit from an additional parent.

COMMENTS AND CRITIQUES:

A really charming little film, the buoyant mood of *The Happy Road* begins as the credits unfold and, on the soundtrack, Maurice Chevalier is heard singing the title song.

In the *Los Angeles Examiner,* Sara Hamilton said it all:

The Happy Road is the right road to travel if you're searching for a highway of good humor, romance and all out entertainment . . . In all departments, Gene Kelly has done a bang-up job. And the warbling of the title song by Maurice Chevalier lends it that one perfect touch.

AN ALLIED ARTISTS PICTURE 1957

With Audrey Hepburn

Produced and Directed by Billy Wilder. Assistant Director, Paul Feyder. Screenplay by Billy Wilder and I. A. L. Diamond. Based on the novel, "Ariane," by Claude Anet. Photographed by William Mellor. Musical Adaptation by Franz Waxman. Musical Editor, Robert Tracy. Sound Recorder, Jo De Bretagne. Sound Editor, Del Harris. Art Direction by Alexandre Trauner. Second Unit Director, Noel Howard. Audrey Hepburn's Costumes by Hubert de Givenchy. Edited by Leonid Azar. Filmed at the Studios de Boulogne in France. 125 minutes.

SONGS:

"Fascination" by F. D. Marchetti and Maurice de Feraudy. "C'est Si Bon" by Henri Betti and André Hornez. "L'âme Des Poetes" by Charles Trenet. "Love in the Afternoon," "Ariane" and "Hot Paprika" by Matty Malneck.

CAST:

Frank Flannagan, GARY COOPER; *Ariane Chavasse,* AUDREY HEPBURN; *Claude Chavasse,* MAURICE CHEVALIER; *Monsieur X,* John McGiver; *Madame X,* Lise Bourdin; *Michel,* Van Doude; *Hotel Guest,* Olga Valery; *The Gypsies:* Gyula Kokas, Michel Kokas, George Cicos, Victor Gazzoli; *Commissioner of Police,* Bonifas; *Brunette,* Audrey Wilder; *Swedish Twins,* Leila and Valerie Croft; *Ritz Valet,* Charles Bouillard; *Ritz Maid,* Minerva Pious; *Porters:* André Priez, Gaidon; *Doorman,* Gregory Gromoff; *Butcher,* François Moustache; *Baker,* Jean Sylvain; *Customers:* Gloria France, Annie Roudier, Jeanne Charblay, Odette Charblay; *Existentialists:* Janine Dard, Claude Ariel; *Undertaker,* Bernard Musson; *Widow,* Michele Selignac; *Artist,* Alexander Trauner; *Rich Women:* Marcelle Broc, Marcelle Praince; *Gigolo,* Guy Delorme; *Generals:* Charles Lemontier, Christian Lude, Emile Mylos; *Cyclists:* Eve Marley, Jean Rieubon; *Lovers:* Gilbert Constant, Monique Saintey, Jacques Preboist, Anne Laurent, Jacques Ary, Simone Vanlancker, Betty Schneider, Georges Perrault, Vera Boccadoro, Marc Aurian; *Husband,* Richard Flagy; *Wife,* Jean Papir; *Children:* Solon Smith, Olivia Chevalier.

STORY:

As Claude Chavasse, a private detective, presents his client, Monsieur X, with evidence that his wife has been indiscreet with Frank Flannagan, an American playboy, Chavasse's daughter, Ariane, eavesdrops outside his office. Then, after Monsieur X leaves, she rushes to Flannagan's suite at the Ritz Hotel to warn him that he is about to be shot by an irate husband. Fascinated with her, Flannagan makes a date to see her again.

After many an afternoon rendezvous with Flannagan, at which she has pretended to be a notorious adventuress, Ariane realizes she is in love with him and cannot continue the charade. Concerned when she fails to keep a date, Flannagan hires her father, unaware of her identity, to find her.

When Chavasse learns the truth, he begs Flannagan to forget his naïve daughter and leave Paris. But as Flannagan is about to leave the depot for a Riviera holiday, Ariane shows up to bid him farewell and he realizes that he cannot leave without her.

With Audrey Hepburn

With Gary Cooper, director Billy Wilder and Audrey Hepburn

With Gary Cooper

COMMENTS AND CRITIQUES:

"Ariane," the novel on which *Love in the Afternoon* is based, was filmed in 1926 and again, under its original title, in 1933 as a vehicle for Elisabeth Bergner. At that time, Maurice Chevalier was Paramount's highest salaried, biggest drawing male star and Gary Cooper was their fastest rising young star. Except for occasional nods-in-passing on various sound stages or at the commissary, Chevalier and Cooper had very little to do with each other. Professionally, of course, they had shared "guest star" billing on two films, *Paramount on Parade* and *Make Me a Star* (and both had worked in the Masquers Club two-reeler, *The Stolen Jools*) but *Love in the Afternoon* was the only film in which they shared scenes.

At Paramount, Chevalier, the foreigner, was usually withdrawn and serious between scenes while Gary Cooper, the young, suddenly sure of himself acting phenomenon, was extroverted and easy-going. During the filming of *Love in the Afternoon* their personalities were altogether switched. Cooper was now the quiet, withdrawn foreigner (this was his first European-made film) and Maurice Chevalier was the seemingly ageless Puck who kept cast and crew in happy spirits. Audrey Hepburn's fascination with Chevalier grew into a lifetime friendship.

Many people, some critics included, did not think Miss Hepburn was as facetious as she meant to be when, after a preview of *Love in the Afternoon,* she said it probably would have been a much more believable film if Chevalier and Cooper had switched roles!

Be that as it may, in the *Hollywood Reporter,* James Powers said:

Chevalier is completely beguiling, a knowledgeable father, at once both a stern parent and an amiable rascal. . . . *Love in the Afternoon* is a delight any time of any day.

In the *Los Angeles Times,* Edwin Schallert said:

Love in the Afternoon brings joy and gladness to the screen. It is the first film to accomplish this result wholly and completely in a long while. . . . Naturally, Chevalier is a triumphant personality, giving besides a superior performance—a complete departure from the old days.

In *The New York Times,* Bosley Crowther said:

The pedestal on which the reputation of Ernst Lubitsch has been sitting all these years will have to be relocated slightly to make room for another one. On this one we'll set Billy Wilder. Reason: *Love in the Afternoon.*

And *New York* magazine said:

I presume it is every man's privilege to fall in love with Audrey Hepburn. She is a tough girl to resist. At the moment, she is appearing in a delightful fantasy called *Love in the Afternoon,* and the object of her affection is Gary Cooper, portraying an aging American roué ensconced at the Paris Ritz. In this one, Miss Hepburn, God bless her, plays the cello, and is the daughter of a Parisian private eye, Maurice Chevalier. The story makes practically no sense, but it is airy and light, and really quite a treat.

And in *Films in Review,* Courtland Phipps said:

From the moment the film begins, with Detective Chevalier atop the monument in the Place Vendome, photographing, with a telescopic lens, Cooper's rendezvous with a married woman in the Ritz, to the moment the film ends with Cooper scooping Hepburn up as his train leaves a station in Paris, *Love in the Afternoon* is amusing, bright and incredible. . . . The oldest member of the cast seems the youngest—the most unchangeable, the most interested, the wittiest, the most interesting—Maurice Chevalier! He is every bit as charming in a derby as he once was in a strawhat, and he carries the burden of this film's mechanics effortlessly and effectively . . . Gary Cooper, of all people, is the roué, and he looks it the few times the camera stays on his once winsome face."

With John McGiver

GIGI

A METRO-GOLDWYN-MAYER PICTURE 1958

With Louis Jourdan and Eva Gabor

With Leslie Caron, Louis Jourdan and Hermione Gingold

Produced by Arthur Freed. Directed by Vincente Minnelli. Screenplay and Lyrics by Alan Jay Lerner. Based on the play, "Gigi," dramatized by Anita Loos from the Colette novel. Photographed in CinemaScope and MetroColor by Joseph Ruttenberg. Music by Frederick Loewe; Supervised and Conducted by André Previn; Orchestrated by Conrad Salinger. Art Direction by William A. Horning and Preston Ames. Set Decorations by Henry Grace and Keogh Gleason. Costumes, Scenery and Production Design by Cecil Beaton. Assistant Directors, William McGarry and William Shanks. Edited by Adrienne Fazan. Filmed at MGM's studios in Culver City, California and on location in France (process photography). 115 minutes.

SONGS:

Maurice Chevalier sings "Thank Heaven for Little Girls," "I'm Glad I'm Not Young Anymore" and a duet with Hermione Gingold, "I Remember It Well." Other songs: "Gigi," "Gossip," "Waltz at Maxim's," "The Night They Invented Champagne," "Say a Prayer for Me Tonight," "It's a Bore" and "The Parisians."

CAST:

Gigi, LESLIE CARON; *Honoré Lachaille,* MAURICE CHEVALIER; *Gaston Lachaille,* LOUIS JOURDAN; *Mme. Alvarez,* Hermione GINGOLD; *Liane d'Exelmans,* Eva GABOR; *Sandomir,* Jacques BERGERAC; *Aunt Alicia,* Isabel Jeans; *Manuel,* John Abbott; *Charles,* Edwin Jerome; *Simone,* Lydia Stevens; *Prince Berensky,* Maurice Marsac; *Show Girl,* Monique Van Vooren; *Designer,* Dorothy Neumann; *Mannequin,* Maruja Ploss; *Redhead,* Marilyn Sims; *Harlequin,* Richard Bean; *Blonde,* Pat Sheehan; *Coachman,* Jack Trevan.

STORY:

Gigi, an illegitimate girl in turn-of-the-century Paris, resides with her grandmother, Mme. Alvarez, and her great aunt, Alicia, who attempt to train her to become a courtesan *par excellence* and, in particular, the mistress of Gaston Lachaille, heir to a sugar fortune.

Beguiled into thinking Gigi will become his mistress and then a carbon of all the other women he has known, the bored and agitated Gaston realizes he loves her and that the only way he can protect her youth and innocence is by marrying her.

Confronted with the first offer of marriage in the entire history of their well-conducted family affairs, Mme. Alvarez, who had once been the mistress of Gaston's uncle, Honoré, finally gives her consent to allow Gigi to marry a desirable man although she's still not certain it's the right thing to do.

With Louis Jourdan and John Abbott

COMMENTS AND CRITIQUES:

A previous version of *Gigi* had been filmed in France in 1950 with Daniele Delorme and the stage production with Audrey Hepburn had captivated New York in 1951, but everyone more or less agreed that the real inspiration for this brilliant musical film was the Lerner-Loewe stage production of *My Fair Lady.* And that *the* inspiration of the film was writing in a part for Maurice Chevalier which, in play and novel, had merely been a character alluded to in passing.

On the night *Gigi* won nine Academy Awards,* Maurice Chevalier was presented with a special Oscar "for his contribution to the world of entertainment for more than half a century."

In *The New York Times,* Bosley Crowther said:

Maurice Chevalier is superb as the cheerful old rip who gets involved in the lively unfolding of the affair. Indeed, M. Chevalier's performance of this tireless boulevardier who views the whole scene of shrewd connivance with full approval and joy is a rare gem of comedy acting—suave, subtle, sensitive and sure. There are those who are ready to name it the most striking thing about the film.

In *Daily Variety,* it was reported:

As might be expected, Chevalier is the scene stealer, at once compelling and at all times the great prophet of French romance. His ageless attraction still proves to be overpowering, and his cocked-hat

With Hermione Gingold

**Gigi's* nine Academy Awards: Best Picture; Best Director (Vincente Minnelli); Best Screenplay (Alan Jay Lerner); Best Color Cinematography (Joseph Ruttenberg); Best Song ("Gigi"—Alan Jay Lerner and Frederick Loewe); Best Scoring of a Musical Picture (André Previn); Best Film Editing (Adrienne Fazan); Best Costume Design (Cecil Beaton); Best Art Direction and Set Decoration (One Award with statuettes to William A. Horning, Preston Ames, Henry Grace and Keogh Gleason).

With Jacques Bergerac and Louis Jourdan

With Louis Jourdan and Leslie Caron

shuffle will endear him to variously aged women wherever *Gigi* plays.

In the *Los Angeles Examiner,* Kay Proctor said:

It is the old master showman, Maurice Chevalier, who steals *Gigi* lock, stock and barrel! The Chevalier of the '30s in verve and inimitable way of singing a song, blended with the Chevalier of the '50s in the natural appearance and sly wit.

Actually Chevalier is the heart and soul of *Gigi,* the genesis of spirit that makes it such wonderful, unusual, unadulterated entertainment.

In the *Saturday Review,* Arthur Knight opined:

Visually, *Gigi* is one of the most elegant and tasteful musicals that MGM has ever turned out. Nor does it lag too far behind musically. . . . Maurice Chevalier carries the major vocal assignments with all the exuberance and charm at his command. And Hermione Gingold combines a vinegary poise with a sugary singing style. Her duet with Chevalier is one of the high points of a highly enjoyable show.

In *Sight and Sound,* David Vaughan said:

The happiest inspiration is undoubtably the addition to the cast of that "elder Lachaille" mentioned in passing by Colette as a former friend of Gigi's grandmother, in the person of Maurice Chevalier. As an elderly boulevardier uncle of Gaston's, he not only presents a contrast to that young man's jaded view of the world, but serves also as a kind of chorus, commenting on the action and embodying the essential hedonism that underlies it. Chevalier's practised but irresistible charm is one of the film's great assets.

In the *Motion Picture Herald,* Charles S. Aaronson said:

A very special word must be accorded the work of Maurice Chevalier, with his fifty years of playing behind him. As the suave, debonair man-about-town, he was never better. He carries the thematic structure of the story, in narrative, personal performance and song, and he appears as the hub of the wheel about which the story revolves.

If a couple of words had to be chosen to satisfactorily describe *Gigi* those two words would have to be "sheer delight."

With Leslie Caron and Louis Jourdan

COUNT YOUR BLESSINGS

A METRO-GOLDWYN-MAYER PICTURE 1959

Produced by Karl Tunberg. Directed by Jean Negulesco. Screenplay by Karl Tunberg. Based on the novel, "The Blessing," by Nancy Mitford. Photographed in CinemaScope and MetroColor by Milton Krasner and George J. Fölsey. Photographic Lenses by Panavision. Music Composed and Conducted by Franz Waxman. Sound Recording Supervisor, Franklin Milton. Art Direction by William A. Horning, Randell Duell and Don Ashton. Set Decorations by Henry Grace and Keogh Gleason. Color Consultant, Charles K. Hagedon. Gowns by Helen Rose. Make-Up by William Tuttle and David Aylott. Hair Styles by Sidney Guilaroff. Assistant Director, William Shanks. Edited by Harold F. Kress. Filmed in England and France. 102 minutes.

With Deborah Kerr

CAST:

Grace Allingham, DEBORAH KERR; *Charles-Edouard de Valhubert,* ROSSANO BRAZZI; *Duc de St. Cloud,* MAURICE CHEVALIER; *Sigismond (Sigi),* Martin Stephens; *Hugh Palgrave,* Tom Helmore; *Sir Conrad Allingham,* Ronald Squire; *Albertine,* Patricia Medina; *Nanny,* Mona Washbourne; *Guide,* Steven Geray; *John,* Lumsden Hare; *Secretary,* Kim Parker; *Tourist,* Frank Kreig.

STORY:

Although a son has been born to them, it takes nine years for Grace and her husband, the Marquis de Valhubert, to get together and live as man and wife. From the moment after their hasty World War II marriage, through years of separation, they have been awaiting the time when they can embark on a honeymoon.

When the time does come, Grace discovers her husband has a mistress as well as several lady acquaintances who are all hoping to qualify for that status if he should become displeased with Albertine. Horrified at first, Grace accepts the situation after her husband's uncle (Duc de St. Cloud) explains that this is a way of life to a Frenchman and no self-respecting one would be without a mistress.

She also discovers their son, Sigi, has been doing his best to keep his parents separated because each overindulges him when the other isn't around. Fearing the worst when his treachery is exposed, Sigi runs away from home. While searching for him, his parents, realizing they love him and each other, are reunited.

Director Jean Negulesco on the set with Chevalier and Deborah Kerr

With Deborah Kerr

COMMENTS AND CRITIQUES:

The best that MGM had to offer Maurice Chevalier after his triumph in *Gigi* was a small but similar role, and star billing, in *Count Your Blessings*. In addition to a handpicked cast, the film had other benisons. Its story was derived from a popular and very witty novel and the production was handsomely mounted, beautifully costumed and designed, and expertly color photographed. It was also booked into Radio City Music Hall. There was just one liability: a dreadfully dull script.

Said the *New Yorker:*

Count Your Blessings, which goes on for better than an hour and a half, had me a trifle uneasy. So did the direction of Mr. Negulesco, who made the thing maunder along to no particular purpose. I forgot to tell you that Mr. Tunberg, the producer, is also responsible for the adaptation of the work. Mr. Tunberg has a lot to account for.

In *The New York Times,* Bosley Crowther said:

With a nod to Nancy Mitford's "The Blessing," which was a good bit more scandalous than this film, he (Karl Tunberg) has knocked out a lightweight diversion that is less notable for wit than for decor.

With Rossano Brazzi, Martin Stephens and Deborah Kerr

CAN-CAN

A 20TH-CENTURY FOX PICTURE 1960

With Louis Jourdan

With Frank Sinatra and Shirley MacLaine

With Frank Sinatra

Produced by Jack Cummings. Directed by Walter Lang. Screenplay by Dorothy Kingsley and Charles Lederer. Based on the stage musical by Abe Burrows. Photographed in Todd-AO and Technicolor by William H. Daniels. Music and Lyrics by Cole Porter. Musical Arranger and Conductor, Nelson Riddle. Choreography by Hermes Pan. Art Direction by Lyle Wheeler and Jack Martin Smith. Set Decoration by Walter M. Scott and Paul S. Fox. Costumes by Irene Sharaff. Edited by Robert Simpson. A Suffolk-Cummings Production. Filmed at the 20th-Century Fox Studios in Century City, California. 134 minutes.

SONGS:

"C'est Magnifique," "It's All Right with Me," "Let's Do It" and "Just One of Those Things" sung by Frank Sinatra. "You Do Something to Me" sung by Louis Jourdan. "Live and Let Live" sung by Maurice Chevalier and Louis Jourdan. "I Love Paris," "Can-Can," "Montmartre" and "Maidens Typical of France" (background instrumentals).

CAST:

François Durnais, FRANK SINATRA; *Simone Pistache,* SHIRLEY MACLAINE; *Paul Barrière,* MAURICE CHEVALIER; *Philippe Forrestier,* LOUIS JOURDAN; *Claudine,* Juliet PROWSE; *André, Headwaiter,* Marcel Dalio; *Orchestra Leader,* Leon Belasco; *Bailiff,* Nestor Paiva; *Photographer,* John A. Neris; *Judge Merceaux,* Jean Del Val; *League President,* Ann Codee; *Chevrolet,* Eugene Borden; *Recorder,* Jonathan Kidd; *Adam,* Marc Wilder; *Policeman Dupont,* Peter Coe; *Plainsclothesman,* Marcel de la Broesse; *Dowagers:* Renée Godfrey, Lili Valenty; *Knife Thrower,* Charles Carman; *Gigi,* Carole Bryan; *Camille,* Barbara Carter; *Renée,* Jane Earl; *Julie,* Ruth Earl; *Germaine,* Laura Fraser; *Gabrielle,* Vera Lee; *Fifi,* Lisa Mitchell; *Maxine,* Wanda Shannon; *Gisele,* Darlene Tittle, *Lili,* Wilda Taylor; *Apache Dancer,* Ambrogio Malerba; *Butler,* Alphonse Martell; *Secretary,* Genevieve Aumont; *Judge,* Edward Le Veque; *Bailiff,* Maurice Marsac.

STORY:

When newly appointed judge Philippe Forrestier announces he will prosecute the owner of any café where the illegal dance, the can-can, is performed he has not yet met Simone Pistache, owner of such an establishment. Protected until now by her attorney, François Durnais, and a sympathetic old judge, Paul Barrière, who never prosecuted her for allowing her girls to dance the can-can, Simone is worried until she meets Philippe and he falls immediately in love.

Simone hopes to use Philippe's marriage proposal as a threat to François, whom she really loves. She is told by François that he doesn't believe lovers should spoil their relationship by getting married. But when he can't discourage Philippe from marrying Simone, even after she has embarrassed him in front of his socialite friends, François is forced to propose marriage with her himself to protect his interests. To preserve hers, Simone accepts.

COMMENTS AND CRITIQUES:

Can-Can got a great deal of pre-release publicity when Soviet Premier Nikita Khrushchev, making a general tour of Hollywood (and 20th-Century Fox Studios in particular) saw some of the completed rushes and watched the climactic dance sequence being filmed. Protocol, however, prevented him from declaring he thought the whole thing was "immoral" until after he was safely off the Fox lot. But while he was a guest of the studio (chosen as the Hollywood site for his historic visit because his favorite actress, Marilyn Monroe, was under contract there) he was wined, dined and introduced to members of the U.S. Royal Family—film stars. Marilyn Monroe was his official hostess for the day —and just so she had something to tell the girls about when she got back to Moscow, Mrs. Khrushchev was given equal rights with Frank Sinatra.

A few days later, when things had calmed down at the Fox studios, Maurice Chevalier, during an interview, said:

> American politicians can learn an important lesson from this occasion. Before too long the candidate seeking office who shows an interest in the performing arts, and can perform himself—especially on television—will be the one who is most successful. Inevitably, of course, all political campaigns will be exercises in acting with the best performer getting the most votes. It has already begun you know, because even now any good politician is a great actor.

When *Can-Can* premiered, as a two-a-day roadshow attraction, most critics contradicted Khrushchev by declaring it was a very circumspect cinemization of the Broadway show.

With Louis Jourdan on the set

Said *Daily Variety:*

A high-kicking ankle-twirling film version of Cole Porter's successful Broadway show. It has a presold title, a box-office cast, a stunning production and a volcano of worldwide prominence from a chunky little man who once visited here from the Soviet Union. Jack Cummings' second film for 20th, it takes its place among the fine motion picture musicals. . . . As a senior judge, Chevalier is the same lovable older-generation spirit he was in *Gigi,* adding refreshing moments to *Can-Can.*

Said *Hollywood Reporter:*

Slow at getting under way, when *Can-Can* hits its stride it whirls like a dervish. . . . Maurice Chevalier is the avuncular confidant of one and all on matters amorous. He claims he is too old for active participation, himself. Nobody believes this for a minute. He's just great.

In *The New York Times,* Bosley Crowther said:

Maurice Chevalier totters meekly on the fringes as an elderly judge who is not so sure in this picture that God should be thanked for little girls, particularly when the creatures are as frightening as Miss MacLaine.

And in the *Los Angeles Examiner,* Ruth Waterbury said:

Can-Can is a valentine of a movie, loaded with color, action, goofy romance, wonderful, wonderful costumes, suspense, laughter and fine performances with Chevalier being the same old delight he was in *Gigi* and playing much the same role. Terrific, this gentleman.

With Frank Sinatra

A MAGNA PICTURES RELEASE 1960

Cyd Charisse

Produced by Joseph Kaufman and Simon Schiffrin. Directed by Terence Young. Photographed in Technirama and Technicolor by Henri Alekan. Edited by Françoise Javet. Filmed in France. 140 minutes. The version edited for U.S. distribution, with English-language narration, is 120 minutes.

STORIES:

Four separate ballets, introduced and occasionally narrated or commented on by MAURICE CHEVALIER.

1: LA CROQUEUSE DE DIAMANTE *(The Diamond Cruncher)*. Ballet by Roland Petit, story by Roland Petit and Alfred Adam. French lyrics by Raymond Queneau. English version by Herbert Kretzmer. Music by Jean-Michael Damase, published by S.E.M.I. Sets and costumes by George Wakhevitch. Cast: The Diamond Cruncher, ZIZI JEANMAIRE; *Pierrot,* DIRK SANDERS.

A fairy tale in which a young lady who rules the Paris underworld discovers it is no fun to crunch diamonds when you can eat cabbages instead with the man you love.

2: CYRANO DE BERGERAC. Ballet by Roland Petit, based on the play by Edmond Rostand. Music by Marius Constant, published by Ricordi. Sets by Bazarte. Costumes by Yves Saint-Laurent. Cast: *Roxanne,* MOIRA SHEARER; *Cyrano,* ROLAND PETIT; *Christian,* GEORGE REICH.

Love letters written by Cyrano to Roxanne, which are supposedly the inspiration of Christian, preclude Cyrano from revealing the truth of his love for her after Christian is killed in battle.

3: DEUIL EN 24 HEURES *(A Merry Mourning).* Ballet and story by Roland Petit. Music by Maurice Thiriet, published by S.E.M.I. Sets and costumes by Antoni Clave. Cast: *The Widow,* CYD CHARISSE; *The Young Man,* ROLAND PETIT; *The Husband,* HANS VAN MANEN.

After chiding his frivolous and beautiful wife for admiring a black gown in a Champs Elysées shop window, her husband is challenged to a duel and killed. He is mourned by his widow, who, in her new black gown, attracts her husband's killer.

4: CARMEN. Ballet by Roland Petit, inspired by the opera, book by Henri Meilhac and Ludovic Halevy, music by Georges Bizet, published by Choudens. Sets and costumes by Antoni Clave. Cast: *Carmen,* ZIZI JEANMAIRE; *Don José,* ROLAND PETIT; *Toreador,* HENNING KRONSTAM.

The classic triangle of the gypsy cigarette girl, the army officer and the bull fighter whose hot-blooded passions lead to cold-blooded murder.

COMMENTS AND CRITIQUES:

Black Tights came at the end of a cycle of ballet films which, starting with *Specter of the Rose,* included *The Red Shoes,* an Academy Award winner, *Tales of Hoffman,* Gene Kelly's financial fiasco *Invitation to the Dance* and his immensely popular Oscar-winning hit, *An American in Paris.* Commercially popular, *Black Tights* was very well received critically.

In the *Los Angeles Herald-Examiner,* George H. Jackson said:

Imaginative in concept, exciting in execution and brilliant in presentation is *Black Tights*. . . . There

is no dialogue in the dance sequences, but Maurice Chevalier is around to tie the episodes together with a narration and also is heard off screen a few times describing what is taking place.

In *Film Daily,* Madel Herbstein said:

A lavish picture of wit, charm and appeal, *Black Tights* twinkles brightly . . . The movie puts together four love stories in ballet form, with the elegant Maurice Chevalier introducing each story with his own mixture of charm and sophistication.

Motion Picture Herald said:

Bubbling, gay and colorful as a boxful of ribbons, this Parisian confection boasts four of the most famous names of the dance world, a happy boulevardier commentary by Maurice Chevalier, magnificent photography in Technicolor and Technirama, and a charm and verve which only the French at their most playful can impart.

Un, Deux, Trois, Quatre!, the 140-minute French version, was originally shown out of competition at the 1960 Venice Film Festival. Most critics thought that version overlong. In *Films in Review,* Francis Koval said:

The opening night of this Venice Festival was as gala as the openings of previous ones. The evening's picture, shown out of competition, was *Un, Deux, Trois, Quatre,* a ballet film made in Paris by Terence Young. It consisted of two gay, and of two dramatic, sketches, charmingly introduced by Maurice Chevalier. The choreography was by Roland Petit and the principal dancers were Cyd Charisse and Zizi Jeanmaire, all three of whom were present. It ran too long, and a highly stylized *Carmen,* illy placed as the end-piece, could cause a riot in Spain. Technirama photography on 70mm stock was technically brilliant.

Roland Petit
and Zizi Jeanmaire

A BREATH OF SCANDAL

A PARAMOUNT PICTURE 1960

With Sophia Loren

Produced by Carlo Ponti and Marcello Girosi. Associate Producer, Gene Allen. Directed by Michael Curtiz. Assistant Director, Mario Russo. Screenplay by Walter Bernstein. Based on Ferenc Molnar's play, "Olympia," adapted by Sidney Howard. Photographed in VistaVision and Technicolor by Mario Montuori. Musical Score by B. Cicognini. Music and Lyrics for the Title Song by Robert Stolz and Al Stillman. Art Direction by Hal Pereira and Eugene Allen. Wardrobe Designed by George Hoyningen-Huene. Edited by Howard Smith. A Ponti-Girosi Production, filmed in Austria and Italy. 98 minutes.

SONG:

"A Smile in Vienna," by Sepp Fellner, Karl Schneider and Patrick Michael, sung by Maurice Chevalier.

CAST:

Olympia, SOPHIA LOREN; *Charlie,* JOHN GAVIN; *Philip,* MAURICE CHEVALIER; *Eugenie,* Isabel JEANS; *Lina,* Angela LANSBURY; *Albert,* Tullio Carminati; *Aide,* Roberto Risso; *Rupert,* Carlo Hintermann; *Can-Can Girl,* Milly Vitale; *Amelia,* Adrienne Gessner; *Count Sandor,* Frederick von Ledebur.

With Milly Vitale

STORY:

While attempting to pressure Princess Olympia into marrying Rupert, a Prussian prince she doesn't love, Olympia's mother, Eugenie, gets no help at all from Philip, her husband, who believes his daughter should make her own decisions about whom she wants to marry.

Subsequently, when Olympia meets an American mining engineer, Charlie, and spends an innocent but romantic night with him at her hunting lodge, Philip, just to pique his wife, is all for spreading this gossip around the court of Emperor Franz Joseph. But Princess Eugenie, using every pressure at hand, including a bit of blackmail, manages to subdue all the whispering.

Not sure she wants everyone at court to think her *that* virtuous, Olympia, with the help of Philip, manages to get Charlie back to her lodge for a three-day weekend. Afterward, she lets everyone at court wonder if it was all as innocent as Charlie declared it was.

COMMENTS AND CRITIQUES:

The most interesting and exciting thing about *A Breath of Scandal* was the magnificent location photography, particularly at Vienna's Belvedere Palace, Prein Castle and Prater Amusement Park.

If you count the Spanish, German, French and English language productions of MGM's 1929 film version of this Molnar play, then called *His Glorious Night,* as separate films, which indeed they were, *A Breath of Scandal* is the fifth time "Olympia" was filmed. This version, with a screenplay based on an adaptation by Sidney Howard, who wrote the screenplay for *Gone With the Wind,* had been planned and postponed by MGM since 1938. They in turn sold it to Carlo Ponti around the time they acquired *Gigi.* All of which helps explain a very curious screen credit on *A Breath of Scandal* for writer Sidney Howard, who had died in 1939 before even *Gone With the Wind* was completed!

With John Gavin and Milly Vitale

In the New York *Times*, Bosley Crowther said:

The most scandalous thing about *A Breath of Scandal* is the fortune squandered in it upon a slip of an idea. Thousands of dollars worth of costumes, buckets of pseudo-Hapsburg jewels, indoor and outdoor settings at some of Vienna's most regal palaces, and a cast headed up by Sophia Loren, John Gavin, and Maurice Chevalier are tossed away on a skinny fable.

And *Weekly Variety* said:

Tis a far, far better world audiences will escape to when they witness *A Breath of Scandal.* Set against the exquisite Austrian countryside and some luxurious Hapsburg interiors, it plants the spectator in a fairytale world of benevolent despots, beautiful princesses and upstart American commoners so handsome and moral it hurts the intellect. . . . Maurice Chevalier is Maurice Chevalier, never managing to submerge his own identity into the character he plays—Miss Loren's father. Nor does it matter.

With Milly Vitale

PEPE

A COLUMBIA PICTURE 1960

Dan Dailey, Maurice Chevalier and Cantinflas

Produced and Directed by George Sidney. Screenplay by Dorothy Kingsley and Claude Binyon. Screen story by Leonard Spigelgass and Sonya Levien, based on the play, "Broadway Magic," by L. Bush-Fekete. Photographed in Panavision, CinemaScope and Pathé Color by Joe MacDonald. Musical Score and Supervision by Johnny Green. Music Editor, Maury Winetrobe. Special Material and Routines by Roger Edens. Sound by James Z. Flaster. Recording Supervisor, Charles J. Rice. Choreography by Eugene Loring and Alex Romero. Art Director, Ted Haworth; associate, Gunther Gerszo. Set Decorator, William Kiernan. Gowns by Edith Head. Makeup Supervisor, Ben Lane. Hair Stylist, Larry Germaine. Associate Producer, Jacques Gelman. Assistant Director, David Silver. Script Supervisor, Marshall Wolins. Edited by Viola Lawrence and Al Clark. Photographic Lenses by Panavision. Print by Technicolor. Filmed in Hollywood and Mexico. 195 minutes.

SONGS:

"The Rumble" instrumental by André Previn. "The Faraway Part of Town" and "That's How It Went, All Right" by André Previn and Dory Langdon. "Pepe" by Hans Wittstutt and Dory Langdon. "Lovely Day" ("Concha Nacar") by Augustin Lara and Maria-Teresa Lara, English lyrics by Dory Langdon. "Hooray for Hollywood" by Johnny Mercer and Richard Whiting, special new lyrics by Sammy Cahn. "September Song" by Kurt Weill and Maxwell Anderson and "Mimi" by Richard Rodgers and Lorenz Hart, sung by Maurice Chevalier.

CAST:

Pepe, CANTINFLAS; *Ted Holt,* DAN DAILEY; *Suzie Murphy,* SHIRLEY JONES; *Auctioneer,* Carlos Montalban; *Lupita,* Vickie Tickett; *Dancer,* Matt Mattox; *Manager,* Hank Henry; *Carmen,* Suzanne Lloyd; *Jewelry Salesman,* Stephen Bekassy; *Waitress,* Carol Douglas; *Priest,* Francisco Reguerra; *Charro,* Joe Hyams; *Dancer,* Michael Callan; *Schultzy,* Ann B. Davis; *Studio Gateman,* William Demarest; *Immigration Inspector,* Ernie Kovacs; *Dennis the Menace,* Jay North; *Bunny,* Bunny Waters; and the voice of JUDY GARLAND.

GUEST STARS (as themselves):

JOEY BISHOP, BILLIE BURKE, MAURICE CHEVALIER, CHARLES COBURN, RICHARD CONTE, BING CROSBY, TONY CURTIS, BOBBY DARIN, SAMMY DAVIS, JR., JIMMY DURANTE, JACK ENTRATTER, COL. E. E. FOGELSON, ZSA ZSA GABOR, GREER GARSON, HEDDA HOPPER, PETER LAWFORD, JANET LEIGH, JACK LEMMON, DEAN MARTIN, KIM NOVAK, ANDRÉ PREVIN, DONNA REED, DEBBIE REYNOLDS, CARLOS RIVAS, EDWARD G. ROBINSON, CESAR ROMERO, FRANK SINATRA.

STORY:

While attempting to keep track of a white stallion to which he is devoted, and which a drunken film director bought at a Mexican auction, Pepe, an ignorant ranchhand, follows the horse and its new owner to Las Vegas and Hollywood, where he eventually ends up producing a movie in which the horse has a featured part.

COMMENTS AND CRITIQUES:

After producer Michael Todd popularized the spectacle film, in which many guest stars make cameo appearances, with his production of *Around the World in 80 Days,* a plethora of such films followed. Of them all, *Pepe,* without a doubt, was the most asinine, patronizing, vulgar and popular imitation.

In *Films in Review,* Ellen Fitzpatrick said:

It seems incredible that anyone with the experience of George Sidney should embark upon a multi-million dollar exploitation of Cantinflas with no better an idea than a feeble imitation of *Around the World in 80 Days*. . . . There are only a few laughs in the three and a quarter hours, and only a few of the 'cameo' performances and stunts come off.

And the *New Yorker* said:

This witless affair deals with a Mexican hayseed, played by Cantinflas, who wanders from his village to such worldly environs as Hollywood, Las Vegas, Acapulco, and Mexico City, in order to be near his beloved horse, which has been sold to a movie director . . . Cantinflas is an attractive and talented fellow, and it is hard to understand why he agreed to identify himself with such a grim disaster as *Pepe.*

Said *Time:*

Pepe goes on and on and on (for 3 hr. 15 min.) until even the hardiest celebrity chaser may get tired of the face dropping. Just screening the titles takes so long that many a viewer will have finished his first box of popcorn before the action starts . . . an oft-told Hollywood tale that was never worth telling in the first place.

FANNY

A WARNER BROS. PICTURE 1961

Chevalier as Panisse

With Horst Buchholz and Charles Boyer

Produced and Directed by Joshua Logan. Associate Producer, Ben Kadish. Assistant Director, Michel Romanoff. Screenplay by Julius J. Epstein. Based on the play, "Fanny"; Book by S. N. Behrman and Joshua Logan; Music and Lyrics by Harold Rome; Produced on the Stage by David Merrick. From the Marseilles Trilogy by Marcel Pagnol. Photographed in Technicolor by Jack Cardiff. Music by Harold Rome. Musical Adaptation by Harry Sukman. Music Supervised and Conducted by Morris Stoloff. Sound by Jean Moncharlon and Richard Vorisek. Art Director, Rino Mondellini. Set Decorator, Robert Turlure. Costume Designer, Anne-Marie Marchand. Makeup by Michael Deruelle. Dialog Coach, Joseph Curtis. Unit Manager, Paul Laffargue. Production Manager, Ludmilla Goulian. A Mansfield Production. Filmed in France. 133 minutes.

CAST:

Fanny, LESLIE CARON; *Panisse,* MAURICE CHEVALIER; *César,* CHARLES BOYER; *Marius,* HORST BUCHHOLZ; *Escartifique,* BACCALONI; *Monsieur Brun,* Lionel Jeffries; *The Admiral,* Raymond Bussières; *Louis Panisse,* Victor Francen; *Honorine,* Georgette Anys; *Cesario,* Joel Flateau.

STORY:

Marius, the son of César, a Marseilles saloon keeper, is loved by Fanny, the daughter of a fishmonger, although he prefers going to sea and finding "the isles beneath the wind" to marrying her. Contriving to trap him, Fanny spends a night with Marius and when she later confronts him with her pregnancy, César insists he marry her. Realizing she has destroyed Marius' dream, Fanny refuses to marry him and says she intends marrying Panisse, a wealthy shopkeeper who has always loved her.

A year later Marius returns and tells Fanny the sea was a disappointment to him and his "isles beneath the wind" turned out to be nothing more than volcanic ash. He begs Fanny to stay with him but César implores him to leave her in peace and never try to see her again.

Some eight years later, Panisse, on his deathbed, has learned of Marius' return to Marseilles and that he works as a garage mechanic. He expresses a dying wish to Marius in a note, begging him to marry Fanny. "I will rest easier knowing she has someone to care for her, especially if it's someone she has always loved. I also feel that my son should have a father, even though it's his own."

With Leslie Caron and Joel Flateau

COMMENTS AND CRITIQUES:

There is absolutely no way anyone can be objective about *Fanny*. It's just one of those rare films you have to see with your heart. Based on Marcel Pagnol's famous stage trilogy of the Marseilles waterfront, it was first filmed as three separate and brilliant French films, *Fanny*, *César* and *Marius*, with the great Raimu. Later MGM made another version *(Port of Seven Seas)* before *Fanny* captivated Broadway as a tuneful musical, courtesy of a Harold Rome score.

For his film version, Joshua Logan presented it as a straight comedy-drama, using the Harold Rome score only as background music. Whatever reservations devotees of the musical may have had when they heard this, one look-and-listen at Logan's *Fanny* convinced them he had done exactly the right thing.

In the *New Yorker*, Brendan Gill said:

Leslie Caron and Horst Buchholz play the troubled young lovers, but it is those fantastic old stagers Charles Boyer and Maurice Chevalier who steal the show. I am ashamed to say it, but in tribute to M. Chevalier I must: In what is surely the most ridiculous deathbed scene ever filmed, Chevalier, playing the dying man, caused me to choke up. A rollicking picture about illicit love, bastardy, and avarice, *Fanny* is ideal for children.

With Horst Buchholz
and Leslie Caron

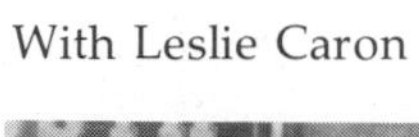

With Leslie Caron

With Georgette Anys

With Leslie Caron

With Lionel Jeffries, Baccaloni and Charles Boyer

Weekly Variety said:

A couple of old pros named Boyer and Chevalier walk off with the picture. Boyer, playing the Raimu role, does it with heart, gusto, humor and manliness—a colorful, compelling portrayal. Chevalier is Chevalier, surely one of the most infectiously lovable and evergreen personalities ever to hit the screen.

In the New York *Times,* Bosley Crowther said:

This charming motion picture, which is legitimately descended from three classic French films of Marcel Pagnol and the Broadway musical, name of *Fanny* based thereon, is a heart-warming splurge of entertainment simply as it stands, without regard for how true it is (or isn't) to the material from which it is derived . . .

It is a fresh and sparkling correlation of a group of people who are individuals in themselves. Mr. Boyer is a raffish, cunning César, but he is also a bit subdued in the face of the jovial, dominating Panisse of Mr. Chevalier. At the same time, Mr. Boyer is full of tenderness and quiet sympathy as the father of the wanderlusting Marius who loves and leaves Fanny to go to sea, and Mr. Chevalier is wonderfully gentle when it comes to wooing and marrying the pregnant girl.

And, in the *Hollywood Reporter,* James Powers declared:

Maurice Chevalier gives the finest performance of his career, genuine acting abetted but not obscured by the fact that he is one of the greatest charmers of our time.

In the *Los Angeles Mirror,* Dick Williams said:

Of the picture's numerous pluses, perhaps the outstanding is Maurice Chevalier's great performance as Panisse, the aging, wealthy sailmaker of the Marseilles waterfront. Chevalier plays a character role, not Chevalier, this time and it may well earn him an Oscar. He is the man to beat.

JESSICA
A UNITED ARTISTS RELEASE 1962

Produced and Directed by Jean Negulesco. Screenplay by Edith Sommers. Based on the novel, "The Midwife of Pont Clery," by Flora Sandstrom. Photographed in Panavision and Technicolor by Piero Portalupi. Musical Score and Songs by Mario Nascimbene, Marguerite Monnet and Dusty Negulesco. Sound Recording by John Kean and Enio Sensi. Art Direction by Giulio Bongini. Assistant Director, Ottavio Oppo. A French-Italian coproduction of Ariane Films and Dear-Film photographed entirely on location in Sicily. 105 minutes.

SONGS:

"It Is Better to Love," "Will You Remember?," "The Vespa Song" and "Jessica" sung by Maurice Chevalier.

CAST:

Jessica, ANGIE DICKINSON; *Father Antonio,* MAURICE CHEVALIER; *Old Crupi,* NOEL-NOEL; *Edmondo Raumo,* Gabriele FERZETTI; *Nunzia Tuffi,* Sylva KOSCINA; *Maria Lombardo,* Agnes MOOREHEAD; *Luigi Tuffi,* Marcel Dalio; *Nicolina Lombardo,* Danielle De Metz; *Gianni Crupi,* Antonio Cifariello; *Virginia Roriello,* Kerima; *Beppi Toriello,* Carlo Croccolo; *Mamma Parigi,* Georgette Anys; *Rosa Mesudino,* Rossana Rory; *Pietro Masudino,* Alberto Rabagliati; *Antonio Risino,* Angelo Galassi; *Filippella Risino,* Marina Berti; *Lucia Casabranca,* Manuela Rinaldi; *Filippo Casabranca,* Gianni Musy; *Rosario,* Joe Polini.

STORY:

Jessica Visconti, an American nurse, works as a midwife in the Sicilian village where her late husband, a doctor, and she had lived and worked before his death. But because the men of Forz D'Agro shout wolf calls to her as she goes by on her motor scooter, the jealous women of the village, led by Maria Lombardo, band together and strike against their husbands. Their logic: if no children are conceived, none will be born; hence, no need for the services of a midwife.

Aware but unperturbed when Father Antonio tells her of the embryogenetic embargo, Jessica hopes to solve the situation by having the handsome widower of a nearby castle, Edmondo Raumi, propose marriage. When he eventually does, the men are resigned and the women are joyous and grateful, although they reluctantly admit the village needs a midwife more than ever. It appears that very few of them lived up to their vows of abstinence and almost all of them are pregnant.

COMMENTS AND CRITIQUES:

Reminiscent of *Lysistrata,* and all its variations, *Jessica* was a showcase production for the abundant physical charms of Angie Dickinson. Had it been produced in the halcyon days of the great star system, it would have catapulted her to interna-

With Angie Dickinson

tional superstardom. But while it was a personal triumph for Miss Dickinson, the coy charm of its script was not always an asset and it was only a moderately successful programmer.

In *The New York Times,* Abe Weiler said:

Aside from its truly effective scenic compensations, *Jessica,* has not come up with anything really new or exciting for a discerning viewer.

As the unwitting temptress, Angie Dickinson is definitely a sight to behold. The role, it should be stated for the record, does not require much beyond physical attributes, and the honey-haired Miss Dickinson, in shorts or tight fitting bodices, undulates through her assignment to perfection. Maurice Chevalier, as the village priest, who is given to strumming a guitar, conversing with his Maker (much like Fernandel as Don Camillo) and handing out gentle bits of matchmaking advice, is, by and large, a mite too cute to be believed.

Weekly Variety disagreed:

Maurice Chevalier breezes through the part of the

village priest with that familiar sunny countenance, and pauses occasionally to narrate or tackle one of several listenable, but undistinguished, ditties.

So did the *Motion Picture Herald:*

Maurice Chevalier is at his charming best as the priest of the village, whose women are unsettled because their husbands cast glances of desire every time the midwife, played by Angie Dickinson, passes by on her motor scooter.

And in *Films in Review,* Louise Corbin (pseudo. for Henry Hart), said:

This French-Italian co-production is a visual delight, and an almost perfect example of how effective old-fashioned movie hoke can still be. It will entertain the sophisticated as well as the witless, and in these days of existentialist despair that's an achievement . . . And Maurice Chevalier, believe it or not, is wholly credible as a blue-eyed priest in Sicily.

Miss Dickinson, as a blonde, is prettier than as a brunette. Also, she seems happier, and the wound that was once visible in her eyes is now much less so. Her good looks, her good figure, and her new amiability, are a pleasure to see.

But, in the *New Yorker,* Brendan Gill was most discouraging. Said he:

A thoroughly preposterous story about a young American widow who comes to a Sicilian village to serve as a midwife and whose beauty causes all the local males to go mad with desire, it has dialogue that is wooden only when it isn't leaden, and a plot that could have been glued together out of matchsticks by a ten-year-old. As for the casting, Miss Angie Dickinson plays the midwife, and though she is certainly presentable, I kept ungallantly wondering whether it wasn't her motor scooter that the males coveted, deep down in their sensible Mediterranean hearts. The part of the elderly village priest is played by Maurice Chevalier, and for once the saucy old stager looks utterly stumped.

IN SEARCH OF THE CASTAWAYS

A WALT DISNEY PRODUCTION 1962

With Michael Anderson, Jr., Keith Hamshere, Wilfrid Brambell, Wilfrid Hyde-White and Hayley Mills

Associate Producer, Hugh Attwooll. Directed by Robert Stevenson. Screenplay by Lowell S. Hawley. Based on the novel, "The Children of Captain Grant," by Jules Verne. Photographed in Technicolor by Paul Beeson. Music Composed by William Alwyn. Musical Director, Muir Mathieson. Songs by Richard M. and Robert B. Sherman. Sound Editor, Peter Thonion. Sound Recording by Dudley Messenger and Gordon McCallum. Special Effects by Syd Pearson. Special Photographic Effects by Peter Ellenshaw. Art Director, Michael Stringer. Set Dresser, Vernon Dixon. Costume Design by Margaret Furse. Makeup by Harry Frampton. Hairdressing by Barbara Ritchie. Additional Photography by Ray Sturgess, Michael Reed and David Harcourt. Assistant Director, Eric Rattray. Second Unit Director, Peter Bolton. Continuity by Pam Carlton. Production Manager, Peter Manly. Animals by Jimmy Chipperfield. Edited by Gordon Stone. Filmed in England at the Pinewood Studios. Distributed by Buena-Vista. 100 minutes.

With Keith Hamshere and Hayley Mills

SONGS:

"The Castaways Theme," sung by Hayley Mills, accompanied on the guitar by Michael Anderson, Jr. "Merci Beaucoup," sung by Maurice Chevalier. "Grimpons!," sung by Chevalier and Keith Hamshere. "Enjoy It," sung by Chevalier, Mills, Hamshere and Anderson, Jr.

CAST:

Professor Jacques Paganel, MAURICE CHEVALIER; *Mary Grant,* HAYLEY MILLS; *Thomas Ayerton,* GEORGE SANDERS; *Lord Glenarvon,* WILFRED HYDE-WHITE; *John Glenarvon,* Michael ANDERSON, JR.; *Thalcave,* Antonio Cifariello; *Robert Grant,* Keith Hamshere; *Bill Gaye,* Wilfrid Brambell; *Captain Grant,* Jack Gwillim; *Guard,* Ronald Fraser; *Maori Chief,* Inia Te Wiata. Others in the cast: Norman Bird, Michael Wynne, Milo Sperber, Barry Keegan, George Murcell, Mark Dignam, David Spenser, Roger Delgado, Maxwell Shaw and Andreas Malandrinos.

STORY:

Sometime last century, on the strength of an almost illegible note, washed ashore in a bottle, Mary

W-892

With Hayley Mills, Wilfrid Hyde-White and George Sanders

With Hayley Mills

With Wilfrid Hyde-White, Hayley Mills, Keith Hamshere and Wilfrid Brambell

Grant, her brother Robert, shipping baron Lord Glenarvon and his son John, and a whimsical scientist, Professor Paganel, sail for South America in search of the Grant children's father, a shipwrecked sea captain.

After landing, they experience an earthquake in the Andes. Then, while crossing the Pampas, the expedition is attacked by a giant condor. Rescued by Thalcave, an Indian chief, they are caught in the crocodile-infested waters of a flash flood before discovering they have read the note wrong and should be looking for Captain Grant in Australia.

Once there, they are captured by Maori cannibals, who are also holding Captain Grant. Attempting a getaway, the prisoners inadvertently provoke an avalanche which starts a volcanic eruption. They all manage to escape that holocaust in time to fight off the avaricious Ayerton and his mutineers before returning to England.

COMMENTS AND CRITIQUES:

In the tradition of high standards in "family entertainment," which is the trademark of a Walt Disney Production, *In Search of the Castaways,* was a well-produced and well-received feature. By composing the songs Maurice Chevalier sang in this film, Richard M. and Robert B. Sherman, continued a family tradition: their father, songwriter Al Sherman, composed "Livin' in the Sunlight, Lovin' in the Moonlight," and other songs popularized in the 1930s by Maurice Chevalier.

In the *Los Angeles Times,* John L. Scott said:

It would be a strange holiday season without a new Walt Disney motion picture. This year Walt's Yule package—one that most kids will enjoy vociferously—is Jules Verne's adventure tale, *In Search of the Castaways.* The new movie takes 16-year-old Hayley Mills, 73-year-old Maurice Chevalier (who jumps around like a 16-year-old), Wilfrid Hyde-White and two young lads, Michael Anderson, Jr. and Keith Hamshere, on a rousing, globe-circling adventure to find a lost sea captain.

And *Weekly Variety* said:

Thesping is done throughout with a tongue in the cheek exuberance which suggests that Disney and Stevenson have given the actors the go ahead to have fun. At times it almost looks as if they are making up the situations and dialogue as they go along. Maurice Chevalier as the scientist and Wilfrid Hyde-White as the ship owner particularly ham it up most engagingly. Although both look as if they are not taking their chores very seriously, the end product is a couple of very astute, pleasant performances.

A PARAMOUNT PICTURE 1963

With Joanne Woodward

With Joanne Woodward

Produced, Directed and Written by Melville Shavelson. Photographed in Technicolor by Daniel L. Fapp. Color Consultant, Hoyningen-Huene. Musical Score by Leith Stevens. Additional Themes by Erroll Garner. Sound Recording by John Cartier. Art Direction by Hal Pereira and Arthur Lonergan. Set Decoration by Sam Comer and James Payne. Costumes by Edith Head. Paris Originals in the Fashion Show sequence by Christian Dior, Lanvin-Castille, Pierre Cardin and Yves Saint-Laurent. Makeup by Wally Westmore. Assistant to the Producer, Hal Kern. Production Manager, Andrew J. Durkus. Assistant Director, Arthur Jacobson. Filmed in Hollywood, New York and Paris. A Denroc Production. 110 minutes.

SONGS:

"A New Kind of Love," sung during the credits by Frank Sinatra. "Louise" and "Mimi" sung by Maurice Chevalier.

CAST:

Steve Sherman, PAUL NEWMAN; *Samantha Blake,* JOANNE WOODWARD; *Lena O'Connor,* THELMA RITTER; *Felicianne Courbeau,* Eva GABOR; *Joseph Bergner,* George Tobias; *Harry Gorman,* Marvin Kaplan; *Albert Sardou,* Robert Clary; *Suzanne,* Jan Moriarty; *Airline Hostess,* Joan Staley; *Chalmers,* Robert F. Simon; *Floor Walker,* Ted Mapes; *Shoppers:* Gladys Roach, Galen Keith Dahle, Minnie C. Logan, Virginia Carr, Jean Argyle, Mildred Shelton, Emily LaRue, Audrey Swanson and Kay Armour; *Models:* Allyson Daniell, Marylu Miner, Annabelle George, Pat Jones, Allyn Parsons, Gabrielle, Sondra Teke and Christian Kay; *Onlooker,* Army Archerd; *Amazons,* June Smaney, Audrey Betz and Irene Chapman; *Gendarme,* Albert Carrier; *French Waitress,* Jacqueline May; *Waiter,* George Nardelli; *Hansom Cab Driver,* Lomax Study; *Reporter,* Gene Ringgold; *Parisienne Poule,* Laurie Mitchell; *2nd French Girl,* Patricia Olson. Guest Star: MAURICE

CHEVALIER (as himself). Also in the cast: Ralf Harolde, Danielle Aubry, Patricia Howard, Trude Wyler, Judy Garwood, Leno Jo Francen, Anne Ross, Joan Waddell, Vicki Poure, Helen Marler, Mabel Smaney, Alphonse Martell, George Bruggeman, Celeste Yarnall, Francine York, Eugene Borden, Francis Ravel, Valerie Varda, Sue Casey, Suzanne Dadolle, and, as themselves: Jimmy Starr, Peter Canon, and Vern Scott.

STORY:

Fashion expert Samantha ("Sam") Blake, herself a drab dresser, tries to avoid a wolfish columnist, Steve Sherman, whom she has met while enroute to Paris for the latest fashion showings. But, on St. Catherine's Day, the patron saint of all virgins over twenty-five advises her to turn on the glamour, forsake spinsterhood if necessary, but trap Steve.

COMMENTS AND CRITIQUES:

In the last paragraph of their disparaging review, *Time* magazine just about summed up everyone's feelings.

Married since 1958, Stars Newman and Woodward here celebrate their fifth picture together. They are an attractive and talented pair, but the Lunts in their heyday could not have saved this one. So many men's-room jokes to memorize. So many interludes of leaden-footed fantasy to plough through. If *A New Kind of Love* didn't take the magic out of their marriage, Mr. and Mrs. Newman are odds-on to become the sweetest little old couple in Hollywood.

Dream sequence with Joanne Woodward and Paul Newman

PANIC BUTTON

A YANKEE PRODUCTION, DISTRIBUTED BY GORTON ASSOCIATES 1964

With Akim Tamiroff

Produced by Ron Gorton. Directed by George Sherman. Screenplay by Hal Biller. Based on a story by Ron Gorton, dramatized by Gorton and Mort Friedman. Photographed by Enzo Sarafin. Music and Lyrics by Georges Gavarantz. Filmed in Italy. 90 minutes.

CAST:

Phillipe Fontaine, MAURICE CHEVALIER; *Louise Harris,* ELEANOR PARKER; *Angela,* JAYNE MANSFIELD; *Frank Pagano,* Michael Connors; *Pandowski,* Akim Tamiroff; *Guido,* Carlo Croccolo; *Mario,* Vincent Barbi.

SONGS:

"I Can't Resist the Twist" and "It's Spring Every Day" sung by Maurice Chevalier.

STORY:

Phillipe Fontaine, a has-been film star whose old movies have the lowest rating of any shown on television, is hired by Frank Pagano to star in a tv pilot film based on *Romeo and Juliet.* To assure failure, because Pagano Enterprises needs a half-million dollar tax write-off, a seedy dramatic coach, Pandowski, is hired as director and a soft-hearted, high-priced call girl, Angela, is engaged as leading lady.

When the film is completed, Fontaine, who lives in a women's hotel operated by his ex-wife, Louise, learns of Pagano's reasons for making the film. Thinking it contains his greatest dramatic performance, he steals a print of it and enters it in a television film festival where it wins an award—for comedy!

A sponsor offers Pagano two million dollars to turn it into a series which causes him to put his board of directors to work reading every bad script they can find to determine if one is unworthy enough to be their next production.

COMMENTS AND CRITIQUES:

Asked how he liked working with sex symbol Jayne Mansfield, Maurice Chevalier said:

It was most enjoyable. Some smart producer should exploit her comedy potential because she really has a flair for *outré* humor. There's nothing phony about it either. When we were rehearsing a dance scene where we do the Twist—now that's a dance that's ruined people half my age—her bra broke. She stopped to make adjustments, looked around, and said to me, "Things like this happen to me all the time. And always at rehearsals—damn it."

Panic Button had no major release in the U.S. and when it played in the Los Angeles area it was on the lower half of a double bill. It was trade shown in New York and reviews were favorable. *Film Daily* said:

A zany comedy on picture making in Italy that bubbles with humor. *Panic Button* gallops merrily along, turning up bursts of comedy amid touches of corn.

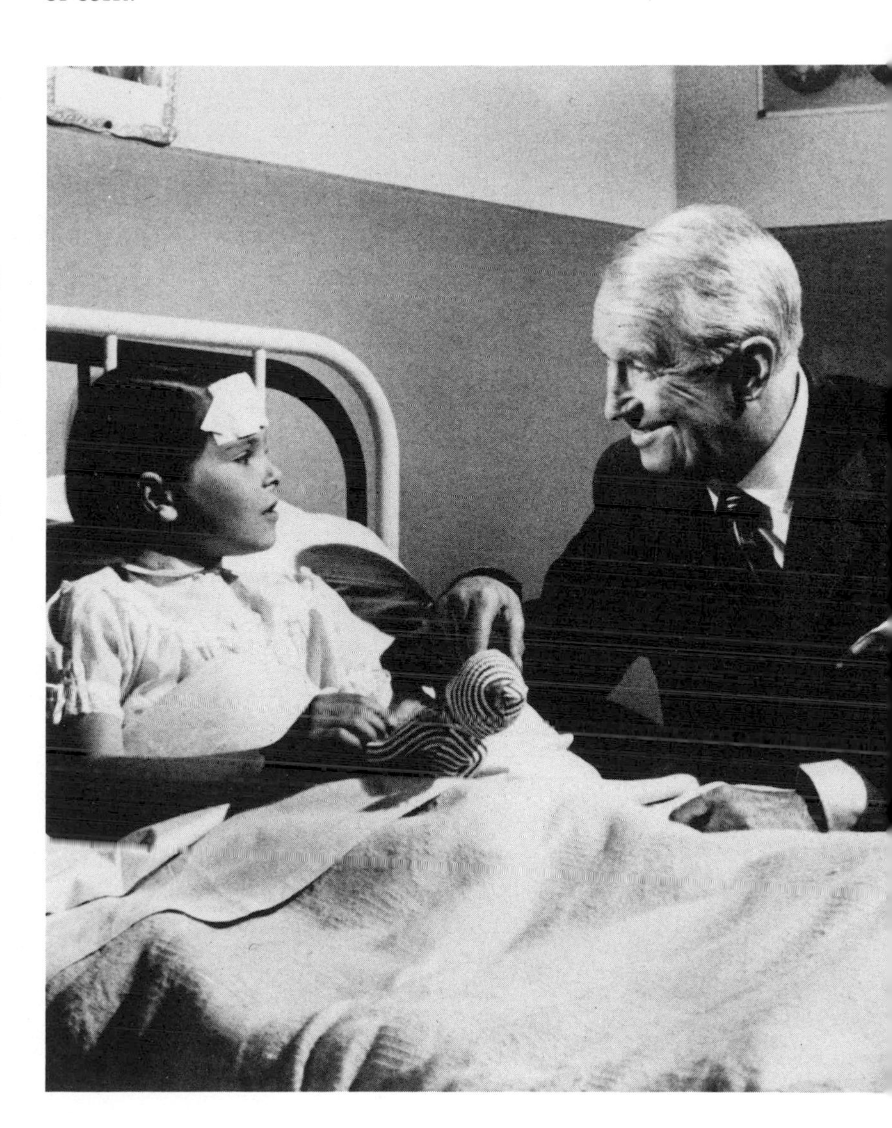

With Michael Conners and Eleanor Parker

The *Motion Picture Herald* said:

This is an enjoyable comedy loaded with the ingredients that make for effective traffic at the box-office. It contains a splendid cast, a zany story embellished with music, and a well mounted production encompassing some fine scenes in Rome and Venice.

In the Los Angeles *Bridge News,* co-author Gene Ringgold said:

If you rummage through enough double bills you occasionally run into a pleasant surprise. *Panic Button* is one of them. Casting Maurice Chevalier, the youngest leading man I can think of, as a washed-up actor and buxom Jayne Mansfield in a comedy about making *Romeo and Juliet* into a tv pilot is a moderately funny idea to which, bless my soul, even Miss Mansfield contributes a couple of deliciously amusing—bits.

I'D RATHER BE RICH

A UNIVERSAL PICTURE 1964

With Hermione Gingold

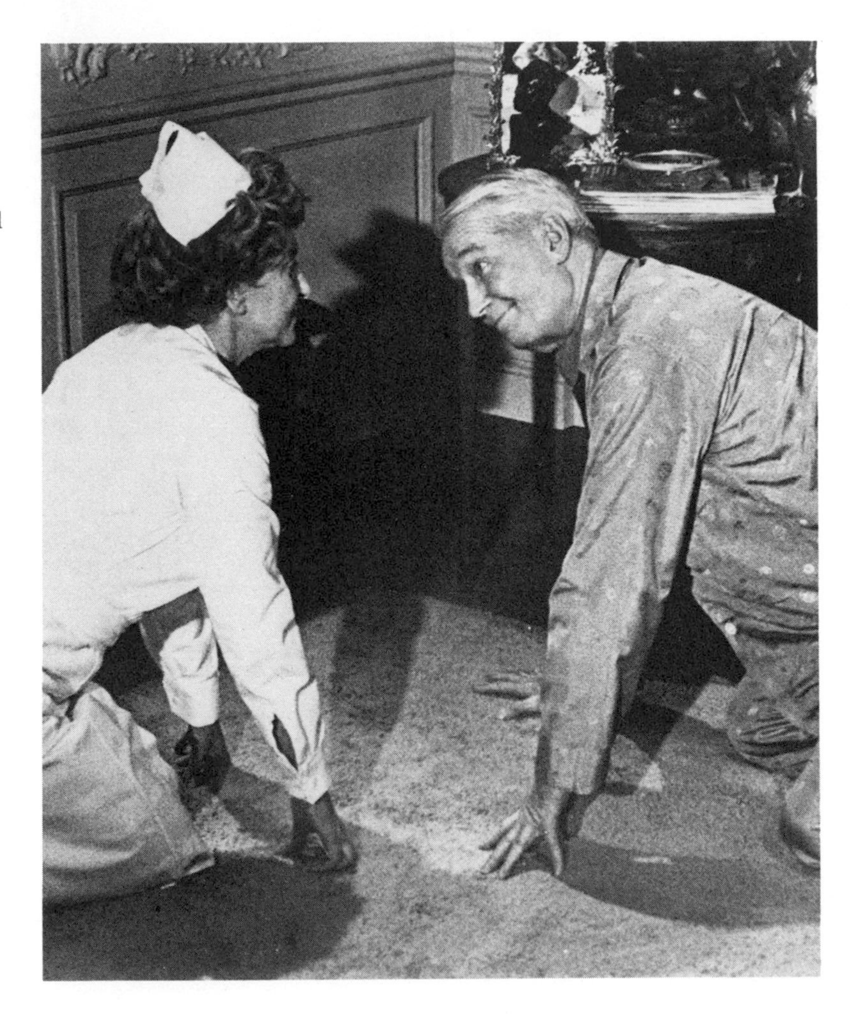

With Hermione Gingold

With Sandra Dee

Produced by Ross Hunter. Directed by Jack Smight. Written by Oscar Brodney, Norman Krasna and Leo Townsend. Photographed in Eastman Color by Russell Metty. Music by Percy Faith. Musical Supervision by Joseph Gershenson. Sound by Waldon O. Watson and Corson Jowett. Choreography by Miriam Nelson and Hal Belfer. Art Direction by Alexander Golitzen and George Webb. Set Decorations by Howard Bristol. Gowns Designed by Jean Louis. Jewels by Cartier. Furs Executed by Alixandre. (Empress Chinchilla Norwegian Saga Fox by Georges Kaplan.) Shoes by David Evins. Leather Outfits by Laura Johnson and Samuel Robert. Makeup by Bud Westmore. Hair Stylist, Larry Germain. Assistant Director, Phil Bowles. Edited by Milton Carruth. Filmed in Hollywood. 96 minutes.

SONGS:

"Almost There" (by Jerry Keller and Gloria Shayne), "Where Are You?" (by Harold Adamson and Jimmy McHugh), "It Had to Be You" (by Gus Kahn and Isham Jones), sung by Andy Williams. "I'd Rather Be Rich" (by Richard Maltby, Jr. and David Shire), sung over main titles by Robert Goulet and Andy Williams. (Reprised over final titles by Goulet, Williams and Maurice Chevalier.)

CAST:

Cynthia, SANDRA DEE; *Philip Dulaine,* MAURICE CHEVALIER; *Paul,* ROBERT GOULET; *Warren,*

With Sandra Dee and Robert Goulet

ANDY WILLIAMS; *Dr. Crandall,* Charlie RUGGLES; *Martin Wood,* Gene RAYMOND; *Miss Grimshaw,* Hermione GINGOLD; *Fred,* Allen Jenkins; *Airlines Clerk,* Rip Taylor; *Harrison,* Laurie Main; *Albert,* Dort Clark; *Cartwright,* Alex Gerry; *MacDougall,* Hayden Rorke; *Mrs. MacDougall,* Jill Jackson; *Max,* Milton Frome; *Directors:* George Milan, Dick Ryan; *First Hunter,* Ben Lessy; *Herself,* Carol Lawrence; *Clergyman,* Jonathan Hole; *Elderly Maid,* Dorothy Neumann; *Second Hunter,* Edward Holmes; *Stockholders' Wives:* Ruth Clifford, Georgine Cleveland; *Directors:* Robert Riordan, Kenneth Patterson, Austin Green and Charles Bell; *Reporter,* Paul Lukather; *Housewife,* Lucille Fenton; *Maitre D',* Richard Flato; *Policeman,* Stuart Wade; *Husband,* Jack Orrison; *Waiter,* Paul Micale; *Reporters:* Richard McGrath, Ray Kellogg, Lincoln Demyan, Bob Duggan.

STORY:

On his deathbed, Philip Dulaine's last wish is to meet his granddaughter Cynthia's fiancé, Warren. But when Warren's plane is fog-bound, Cynthia, fearing the end is near for her grandfather, brings home Paul, whom she introduces as Warren.

Warren's arrival has everyone contriving to keep Dulaine, who has made a miraculous recovery, from meeting him. But Dulaine learns the true identity of each and determines that Paul, not Warren, is the man for his granddaughter to marry. He then goes about making Paul and Cynthia realize this too.

COMMENTS AND CRITIQUES:

Although most of Ross Hunter's movies are nothing more than extravagant shopping sprees where, for very little, audiences can marvel over the latest in fashions and home furnishings without ever feeling an urge to buy anything, including the plot, *I'd Rather Be Rich* seemed much sounder of script than the usual Ross-opera. There was good reason for this since it was a switch-of-gender remake of one of 1941's brightest and most polished comedies, *It Started with Eve,* which had starred Deanna Durbin, Charles Laughton and Robert Cummings.

But even the combination of Ross Hunter and Sandra Dee, which could often turn back the hands of *Time,* did not do so here. Said they:

There must be some mistake—this can't be a good movie. It was produced by Ross Hunter, a man who makes bad movies *(Magnificent Obsession, Imitation of Life)* on principle—the principle that most moviegoers are housewives and most housewives don't care if the story is dull so long as the furniture is interesting. What's more, the picture stars Sandra Dee, a young woman who looks like everything the sociologists say is wrong with American teenagers and acts as though she can't wait to get the picture over with and count her salary.

Nevertheless, *Rich* is a good movie—essentially because Producer Hunter hired a talented TV director named Jack Smight, and Smight makes right. He makes, in fact, a continually lively and sometimes raucously hilarious situation comedy in which two hearty old-timers (Maurice Chevalier,

Hermione Gingold) and two vigorous newcomers (Robert Goulet, Andy Williams) really bust up the producer's fancy furniture and even manage to make Sandra sometimes act like an actress instead of a sick kid with the Dee tease.

But in the *New Yorker*, Brendan Gill gave one of the few negative reports:

I should make it clear that no power under heaven could have turned *I'd Rather Be Rich* into a pleasurable experience. The writers of the leaden script —Oscar Brodney, Norman Krasna and Leo Townsend—have seen to that by their reworking of a thirty-times-told tale of lovers' quarrels and false identities, and they have been backed to the hilt in their fatuity by the director, Jack Smight, who is rumored to have been chosen to direct the forthcoming Biblical epic *Hip and Thigh*. Besides Miss Dee and Mr. Goulet, the large, frightened cast includes a young singer named Andy Williams, a venerable singer named Maurice Chevalier, and those old stagers Hermione Gingold, Gene Raymond, and Charlie Ruggles. Actors like to keep busy, and who can blame them?

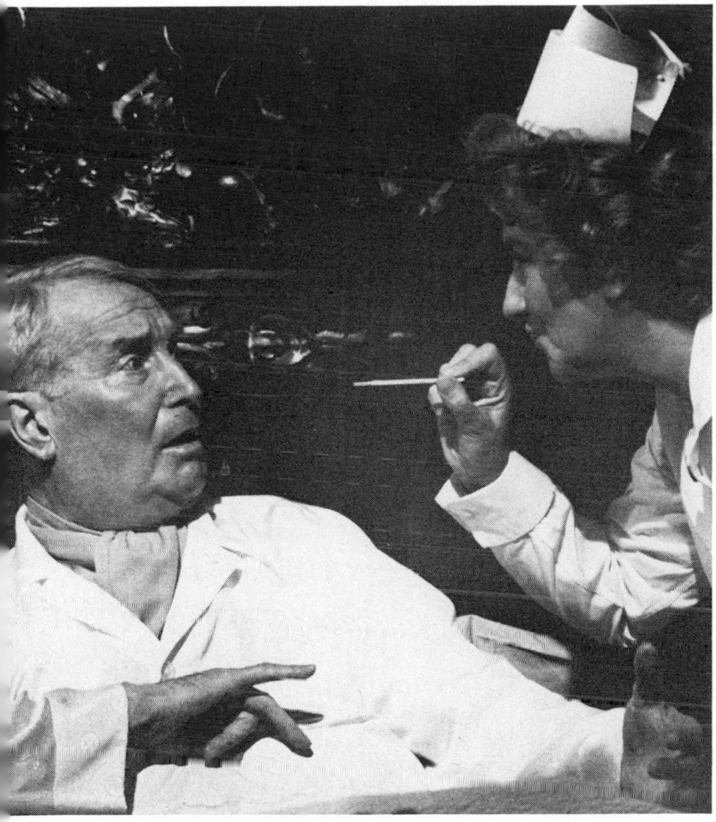

With Hermione Gingold

MONKEYS, GO HOME!

A WALT DISNEY PRODUCTION 1967

With Darlene Carr

Co-Producer, Ron Miller. Directed by Andrew V. McLaglen. Screenplay by Maurice Tombragel. Based on the novel, "The Monkeys," by G. K. Wilkinson. Photographed in Technicolor by William Snyder. Music by Robert F. Brunner, Robert B. and Richard M. Sherman. Orchestrations by Cecil A. Crandall. Music Editor, Evelyn Kennedy. Sound Supervisor, Robert O. Cook. Sound Mixer, Robert Post. Art Direction by Carroll Clark and John B. Mansbridge. Set Decoration by Emile Kuri and Frank R. McKelvy. Costumes Designed by Bill Thomas. Costumers, Chuck Keehne and Neva Rames. Makeup by Pat McNalley. Hair Stylist, La Rue Matherton. Animal Supervision by Stewart Raffill. Dialogue Supervisor, Flora Duane. Assistant to the Producer, Louis Debney. Assistant Director, Tom Leetch. Edited by Marsh Hendry. Filmed at the Disney Burbank studio (California). Distributed by Buena-Vista, Inc. 101 minutes.

SONGS:

"Monkeys, Go Home!" and "Joie de Vivre" sung by Maurice Chevalier (and the school children).

CAST:

Father Sylvain, MAURICE CHEVALIER; *Hank Dussard,* DEAN JONES; *Maria Riserau,* YVETTE MIMIEUX; *Marcel Cartucci,* Bernard Woringer; *Emile Paraulis,* Clement Harari; *Yolande Angelli,* Yvonne Constant; *Mayor Gaston Lou,* Marcel Hillaire; *M. Piastillio,* Jules Munshin; *Grocer,* Alan Carney; *Sidoni Riserau,* Darleen Carr.

With Dean Jones and Bernard Woringer

STORY:

When former astronaut Hank Dussard imports four trained female chimpanzees to harvest the olive crop on the French farm he has inherited, the scheme provokes the ire of the villagers. Led by a real estate agent, Emile Paraulis, and the local butcher, Marcel Cortucci, whose girl friend, Maria, is attracted to Hank, they plot to prevent the simians from harvesting the olives by importing a male chimpanzee to divert the workers.

Father Sylvain, the local priest, who had helped train the monkeys to pick the olives, persuades the villagers to help with the harvest and thereby earn the gratitude of the American interloper instead of devising more schemes for driving an enterprising citizen away.

With Yvette Mimieux and Dean Jones

COMMENTS AND CRITIQUES:

As usual, this Walt Disney production was ideal family fare and very popular. But the Disney trademark may have been a detriment to some so-called sophisticated filmgoers. If so, it's their misfortune. They missed seeing a very expertly made and hilariously funny comedy, free of the saccharine sentiments which disfigure many Disney products.

Maurice Chevalier worked in *Monkeys, Go Home!* during his sixty-eighth year in show business and it is the film which contains his last on-screen performance.

Said *Weekly Variety:*

Chevalier, a showbiz legend, again scores in projecting a benign worldliness. Whether cast as a priest, as here, or else as an engaging man of the world, Chevalier never fails to project the image of a man who has lived fully and learned something positive from the experience.

In the *Hollywood Reporter,* James Powers said:

Maurice Chevalier, as the village priest, gives great strength and sympathy to the film. He breaks into song occasionally, and this is threaded unobtrusively and agreeably into the framework.

In *Films in Review,* Gwenneth Britt said:

Is it difficult for you to admit that Maurice Chevalier will soon celebrate his 80th birthday? Take a look at him in this Disney-made entertainment for children. He plays an amiable priest in a small French village and his smile is as winning as ever.

And *Boxoffice,* which presented it with their "Blue Ribbon Award" as a merit of its entertainment value as family fare, said:

Once again Walt Disney used sure-fire audience ingredients in a wild and wacky comedy which has something to entertain all ages, from the youngsters to mature patrons. The kiddies will delight in the mischievous antics of four girl chimpanzees, the teenagers will be attracted by Dean Jones and Yvette Mimieux, who take care of an American-French romance in pleasing fashion, and, for the oldtimers, there's the incomparable veteran Maurice Chevalier, with his Gallic charm, who also sings "Joie de Vivre" with a children's chorus. That the picture is pleasing first-run audiences in key cities is indicated by its boxoffice score of 196 per cent.

With Dean Jones

A WALT DISNEY PRODUCTION 1970

Chevalier came out of retirement to record the title song

Hermione Baddeley as Madame Bonfamille

Maurice Chevalier with director Wolfgang Reitherman

Ruth Buzzi as Frou Frou

Produced by Wolfgang Reitherman and Winston Hibler. Directed by Wolfgang Reitherman. Story by Larry Clemmons, Vance Gerry, Ken Anderson, Frank Thomas, Eric Cleworth, Julius Svendsen, Ralph Wright, Tom Rowe and Tom McGowan. Directing Animators, Milt Kahl, Ollie Johnston, Frank Thomas and John Lounsbery. Production Designer, Ken Anderson. Character Animation, Hal King, Eric Larson, Eric Cleworth, Julius Svendsen, Fred Hellmich, Walt Stanchfield and Dave Michener. Background Animation by Al Dempster, Bill Layne and Ralph Hulett. Layout by Don Griffith, Basil Davidovich and Sylvia Roemer. Animation Effects by Dan MacManus and Dick Lucas. Processed in Technicolor. Music by George Burns. Orchestrations by Walter Sheets. Music Editor, Evelyn Kennedy. Songs by Richard M. and Robert B. Sherman, Terry Gilkyson, Floyd Huddleston and Al Rinker. Sound by Robert O. Cook. Production Manager, Don Duckwall. Assistant Directors, Ed Hansen and Dan Alguire. Edited by Tom Acosta. Distributed by Buena-Vista, Inc. Created at Walt Disney's Burbank studio. 78½ minutes.

SONGS:

"The Aristocats," sung by Maurice Chevalier. "She Never Felt Alone," "Thomas O'Malley Cat," "Scales and Arpeggios" sung by Phil Harris. "Ev'rybody Wants to Be a Cat" sung by Scatman Crothers.

VOICE TALENTS:

Title Song, MAURICE CHEVALIER; *Scat Cat,* SCATMAN CROTHERS; *Chinese Cat,* PAUL WINCHELL; *English Cat,* LORD TIM HUDSON; *Italian Cat,* VITO SCOTTI; *Russian Cat,* THURL RAVENSCROFT; *Berlioz,* DEAN CLARK; *Marie,* LIZ ENGLISH; *Toulouse,* GARY DUBIN; *Frou Frou,* NANCY KULP; *Napoleon,* PAT BUTTRAM; *Lafayette,* GEORGE LINDSAY; *Abigail,* MONICA EVANS; *Amelia,* CAROLE SHELLEY; *Lawyer,* CHARLES LANE; *Madame,* HERMIONE BADDELEY; *Butler,* RODDY MAUDE-ROXBY; *Uncle Waldo,* BILL THOMPSON; *O'Malley,* PHIL HARRIS; *Duchess,* EVA GABOR; and *Roquefort,* STERLING HOLLOWAY.

STORY:

Edgar, the butler, overhears Madame Bonfamille tell her attorney, Monsieur Hautecourt, she is leaving her estate to her cat, Duchess, and her kittens, and directs him to make out her will accordingly. She also mentions that it is her wish to have the estate pass on to Edgar in the event that the cats should die.

Avaricious, but incapable of murder, Edgar drugs the cats and dumps them in the country, thinking they will be lost forever. But the following morning

Eva Gabor as Duchess

Thomas O'Malley, an alley cat, encounters the Duchess and her brood and, before returning them home, takes them to a jam session where Scat Cat and his hepcats are appearing. Edgar makes one further attempt to dispose of the feline family but they are again rescued by O'Malley and Edgar ends up in a trunk—bound for Timbuktu.

COMMENTS AND CRITIQUES:

By contributing his voice talents to the soundtrack of *The Aristocats,* the cartoon feature on which he completed a sixty-two-year film career, Maurice Chevalier had now worked in every existing genre of the motion picture. Name the category—silent/sound; experimental/professional; feature-length/short subject; live-action/animated; factual/fictional; black-&-white/color; period/contemporary; comedy/drama; musical/fantasy; suspense/romance—and at least one Maurice Chevalier film represents it. He also played himself on the screen twelve times (which does *not* include foreign language versions of the same film), and made films in nine different countries in five languages.

Of the last film to which he contributed, *Boxoffice* said:

The last cartoon feature that Walt Disney was personally involved with, in development since 1963 and four years in the making, *The Aristocats* should make a joyous noise all over for Christmas.

And *Motion Picture Herald* said:

The fact that *Aristocats* is the 23rd feature-length animated film to come from Walt Disney Productions is almost enough said. The 22 pictures which have gone before are the best advertisement that Buena Vista could ask in selling *Aristocats* to the public, and this latest film, the last animated feature begun under the supervision of the late Mr. Disney, stands up as another solid piece of family entertainment.

NOTE:

Maurice Chevalier had officially retired from show business a year before he agreed to sing the title song for *The Aristocats.* His reason for doing so: to fulfill a wish that the late Walt Disney had made of wanting Chevalier's voice among those used in a cartoon taking place in France, and notably, Paris. Said Disney: "Where would France, and the rest of the world for that matter, be without Maurice Chevalier to brighten it up?" That's quite a compliment from the genius who left the children of the world a priceless entertainment legacy.

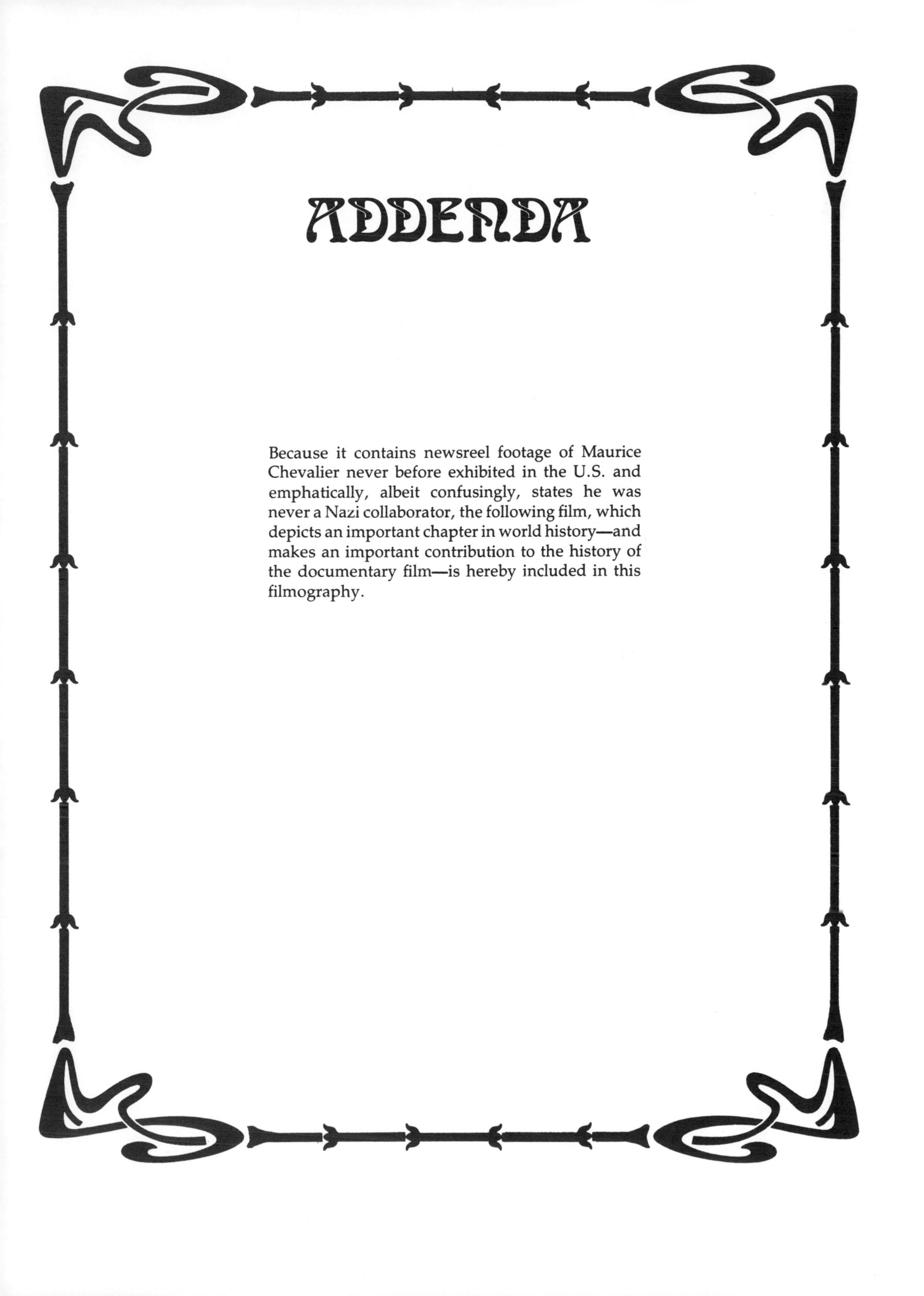

ADDENDA

Because it contains newsreel footage of Maurice Chevalier never before exhibited in the U.S. and emphatically, albeit confusingly, states he was never a Nazi collaborator, the following film, which depicts an important chapter in world history—and makes an important contribution to the history of the documentary film—is hereby included in this filmography.

A CINEMA 5, LTD. RELEASE 1972

Chevalier entertaining the troops

Celebration during the liberation of Paris

Produced and Directed by Marcel Ophuls. Screenplay and interviews by Marcel Ophuls and Andrew Harris. Photographed by André Gazut, Jurgen Thieme and André Juraz. Edited by Claude Vajda. Filmed and Compiled for Television Rencontre-Norddeutscher Rundfunk-Television-Television Swiss Romande, a French, German and Swiss Television Distributor. (Shown in Great Britain and the U.S. with English narration and subtitles.) 260 minutes.

COMMENTS AND CRITIQUES:

This compilation of international newsreel footage of the German Occupation of France during World War II and specially filmed interviews of the supporters of Marshal Pétain, Resistance fighters, collaborationists and members of the German Army, was originally planned for exhibition on German, Swiss and French television. But because the editing and interpretation of the material clearly showed, for the first time, the degeneration and disintegration of all classes of Frenchmen in the time of national crisis it was not telecast in France. It was shown in Germany, Switzerland and England. In order to make it available to the French, it was theatrically exhibited in Paris in a small Left Bank movie house where it caused such a sensation it was transferred to a large theatre on the Champs-Elysées.

The four-hour documentary concludes with an appearance by Maurice Chevalier, at the time of the liberation, noting how he had been rumored to be dead on at least three occasions, and now suggesting that all Frenchmen, who had suffered and lost so much, forgive and forget. He then sings "Sweeping the Clouds Away," the song which he had originally sung in the climax of *Paramount on Parade.*

This footage is so badly edited and juxtaposed—accidentally or purposely?—that some critics (see the excerpt from Alfred Kazin's review in *The New York Times*) were convinced Chevalier was a German collaborator! There is, however, still much truth and power in *Le Chagrin et la Pitié* that is *not* obfuscated by politically biased, or professionally confused editing.

In the *Los Angeles Herald-Examiner,* Bridget Byrne said:

Few come out of this film with any honor. Those who had humanity then have it now. Those who resisted can forgive. Few can admit the wrong they did. Too many turned with the tide to compound their indifference in revenge. Too many speak with the hindsight of politicians, or say "I did not know" when they mean "I didn't dare to ask because I didn't want to know . . ."

The film is not easy viewing. It adds to the sorrows of the living and offers few testimonials to human virtue.

In *The New York Times,* Alfred Kazin said:

When I saw the film here in New York, I was struck by the almost painful attention of so many people around me who had clearly been born after 1945. The Nazi era is a throbbing wound for those not alive during the period because, as any teacher in contact with the young knows, their "nihilism" covers up a good deal of fear of those who were alive then and helped make the period what it was.

The young understand better than we who lived through the war—and who will never recover from it—that human cruelty, human vanity, egotism, selfishness, often express themselves most disgustingly in the form of "national" ideals, as "love of country . . ."

But what happened to so many Frenchmen between 1940–1945 was most often done in the name of "France." Maurice Chevalier is shown on the screen first collaborating, then apologizing; Danielle Darrieux and other movie stars are shown going to Germany to make films. The nightclubs in Paris are shown doing a roaring business while resistance fighters were being tortured in the cellars of the Gestapo.

In *Films in Review,* Charles Phillips Reilly said:

There are some fine moments: Mendès-France narrating how he had to sit on the wall of the prison from which he was escaping because below him on the street a young man was trying to seduce a girl; two teachers in a *lycée* in Clermont-Ferrand who don't even remember that the memorial in the school yard was for boys who died in WWII, not WWI; Dennis Rake, a British agent and homosexual, described by the head of the British underground as one of the bravest of men; and Madame Solange, a beautician who was a victim of the Resistance. Maurice Chevalier at the end explains that he had never collaborated by entertaining Germans in Germany.

This film has received an Academy Award nomination for "Best Documentary," and was a unanimous selection for a special award by the National Society of Film Critics.

NOTE:

Some of the Chevalier footage used in *Le Chagrin et la Pitié* had also been used, to small purpose and no advantage, in two other films: *La Bataille de France,* a 1964 French documentary directed by Jean Aurel; and, *La Naissance,* a 1970 French film, starring Pierre Clementi and Zouzou, directed by Yvan Legrange. At press time of this book, neither film has had a U.S. showing.

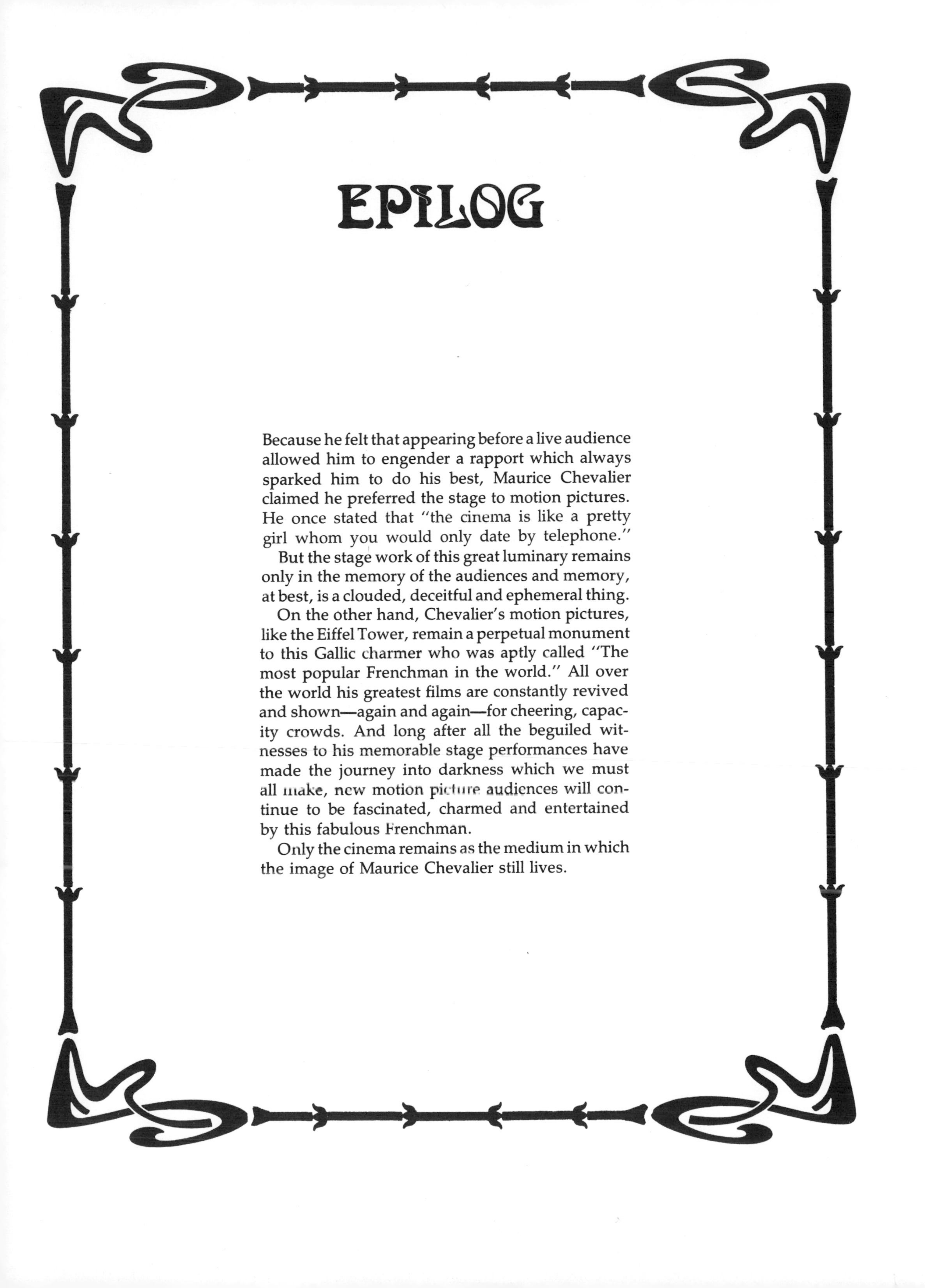

EPILOG

Because he felt that appearing before a live audience allowed him to engender a rapport which always sparked him to do his best, Maurice Chevalier claimed he preferred the stage to motion pictures. He once stated that "the cinema is like a pretty girl whom you would only date by telephone."

But the stage work of this great luminary remains only in the memory of the audiences and memory, at best, is a clouded, deceitful and ephemeral thing.

On the other hand, Chevalier's motion pictures, like the Eiffel Tower, remain a perpetual monument to this Gallic charmer who was aptly called "The most popular Frenchman in the world." All over the world his greatest films are constantly revived and shown—again and again—for cheering, capacity crowds. And long after all the beguiled witnesses to his memorable stage performances have made the journey into darkness which we must all make, new motion picture audiences will continue to be fascinated, charmed and entertained by this fabulous Frenchman.

Only the cinema remains as the medium in which the image of Maurice Chevalier still lives.